Dark Psychology Secrets

How to Analyze & Read People Using Behavioral Psychology, Body Language Analysis, Persuasion & NLP-Signs & Preventive Techniques for Managing Being Manipulated by Toxic People

Table of Contents

Introduction

Have you ever had a moment where you suddenly realized you were doing something that you had not intended to do, and you are not quite sure why you are doing so? Perhaps you have wondered about being able to influence others to behave in ways that would be beneficial to you without having to overtly declare your intentions. You could be a salesperson who will benefit from being able to upsell items to rake in a higher commission. You could be interested in running for politics and want to know how to influence crowds to not only follow but also vote for you. You could even be a manager or owner of a business and want to ensure that you are able to keep everyone under your control and motivated to keep working. Perhaps you fall into the small percentile of people interested in manipulating others for your own selfish interests, such as through seducing another person and molding them into the perfect partner for you.

No matter the reason you have taken an interest in the secrets dark psychology holds, you will not find yourself disappointed. Hidden within the art of dark psychology is the ability to intimately understand the minds of those around you; it provides the skills necessary to really read an individual at a glance, understanding even the most minute of body language to recognize how people are feeling. It teaches you how to behave yourself in conjunction with how others are feeling, understanding such concepts as the principles of persuasion or mirroring, and utilizing them to sway the behaviors of others in return.

With time, effort, diligence, and an eye for detail, you will find that you are capable of influencing and controlling those around you. No, mind control is not just for sci-fi movies—in reading this book, you can actually develop the skills necessary to control the actions of others with ease without them ever realizing what is happening.

As you read through this book, keep your mind wide open to the possibilities. You will be given all of the scientific background you need, with an understanding of emotions and empathy and how they will be recurring themes throughout the entire process. You will learn what makes someone persuasive and how acting with persuasion is different than acting in a manipulative fashion. You will learn how to recognize when others manipulate you, as well as what to look out for in victims of manipulation and how to prevent yourself from falling victim to another person's manipulation. After all, if you are reading this book, you are interested in being the one that is controlling others, not in being controlled. You will learn how to read people, how to use your body language to alter how you appear to those around you, and all about the wondrous secrets of NLP—Neuro-Linguistic Programming, and more.

Regardless of whether you only want to understand influence, persuasion, and manipulation in order to defend yourself or if you want to utilize the skills within these books for yourself, you will gain valuable information that will be able to be used in a wide range of situations. The possibilities are endless.

Chapter 1: What is Dark Psychology?

Psychology on its own is powerful—when you understand how people's minds work, you understand the reasoning behind behaviors. You can see why people would react in the way they did, and also how to expect them to react. Dark psychology is no different—Dark psychology encompasses the study of the minds of those who are ruthless, exploitative, and manipulative. It looks at the minds of the people who are out there to get their own selfish interests met through any means necessary; narcissists, psychopaths, sadists, and other minds that have a tendency toward manipulation have been studied to see what makes them tick, why they do it, and more importantly, how they manage to get others to do exactly what they want.

Dark psychology does not have to be evil, though there certainly are people who use it for that purpose. You can study it to protect yourself—when you understand how it works, you become less susceptible to it. You can use it in genuinely positive manners, such as using your skills in persuasion to benefit someone else. You can use it to get the results you want, or even to get better jobs and perform better socially. Just because people with dark personalities utilize the concepts within dark psychology for selfish uses does not mean you have to go down that same path yourself.

Traits of Dark Psychology

Dark psychology is somewhat unique compared to other schools of psychology, primarily in the fact that it looks solely at insidious behaviors. Its studies manipulation, persuasion, deception, coercion, mind control, and more. It seeks to delve into the minds of those with the darkest personalities, who want to harm others.

These people that make up the central focus of dark psychology are described as evil. They do not care about the people around them, nor does the suffering of others bother them. It also assumes that we all have the potential to end up in that role— we all have a dark side somewhere within us, according to dark psychology, but not everyone chooses to behave that way. While that predatory behavior may lurk within everyone, very few actually want to act with it.

Those who do act upon their dark impulses usually do so to meet some evolutionary, primary instinct. Humans have three: Sex, aggression, and self-preservation. These are survival instincts that are necessary to appeal to survival. Like a pack of wolves, or other carnivorous animals, those who allow their dark sides to rule them hunt with some sort of purpose. They take steps to minimize their own risks, calculating out their moves, and making sure their targets will be easier to overpower. Ultimately, there are six key traits that follow with dark psychology:

- It is universal—all humans have the potential for it

- It looks at how people think and feel about their ability to prey upon others

- It recognizes a spectrum of dark psychology—no two people's behaviors are the same or as harmful

- The spectrum depends on the level of evilness or inhumanity that the perpetrator exhibited in the negative actions

- All people share an innate potential for violent, predatory behaviors

- Awareness of dark psychology and its concepts allow for people to control those impulses while also recognizing that some of the behaviors spurred by dark psychology are evolutionarily developed for survival.

Users of Dark Psychology

Despite the insidious nature of dark psychology, plenty of people use it with far fewer evil intentions. Each category below has a different motivation for utilizing dark psychology, and many of the categories of people use them to better people rather than simply out of selfish desire. The key difference in terms of where it falls in the spectrum is understanding when to use it ethically and when to use it selfishly.

Politicians

Politicians have to be able to read those around them in order to present themselves in ways that are conducive to getting their way. They are able to control their vocal cues, their body language, and behave in ways that come across as confident and authoritative in order to get others to follow them. Their ability to understand human psychology allows them to directly convince others to vote for them or support their causes.

Salespeople

When your job hinges upon selling or convincing other people to sell, understanding how to be persuasive and convince people to listen to what you have to say is crucial. When you can sway others and encourage them to trust your judgment, you will better be able to maximize your own selling potential, ultimately benefitting you more.

Religious leaders

Ultimately, religious leaders want people to follow the rules of their religion. They seek a certain level of obedience and trust, which can be earned through understanding how other people perceive them. Through being able to manipulate their own body language and knowing how to word themselves and persuade others in the most effective manner, religious leaders find themselves far more capable of captivating their audiences and swaying them.

Cults

One of the far more insidious of the example on this list, cults utilize dark psychology and mind control to systematically gain complete and utter control over someone else. They understand the effects of their actions, slowly isolate their targets, and covertly change their mindsets and thoughts, creating perfect pawns that are trapped within their structures.

Lawyers

Especially in court, lawyers have to know how to present themselves. Especially since the court of law requires people to prove something beyond a doubt, the lawyers must be able to present themselves as thoroughly confident in what they are asserting if they hope to get the results they want. For example, an attorney seeking to prove the innocence of their client must be able to wholeheartedly convince others that he believes the innocence of his client, even if he may doubt the client as well.

Narcissists

Egotistical and self-serving, narcissists also utilize dark psychology regularly to systematically browbeat their targets into submission and to achieve anything they may desire as a result. Through dark psychology, they are able to achieve great results, teaching people around them to respond, guilting them into submission, or even just mind-controlling them after some time spent installing the right buttons.

Chapter 2: Emotions

Perhaps the most basic tenet you must understand before approaching dark psychology in any meaningful manner is emotions. You must be able to recognize how emotions sway other people, why we have them, and how to sway them if you want to be able to control people. This is for one key reason—emotions are motivating. They drive everything. Once you understand how people are feeling, you can begin to recognize how your own behaviors influence the feelings of others. Once you understand that, you can tweak your own behaviors intentionally in order to evoke the desired behavior from the other person. The more control you gain over another's emotions, the more control you have over their thoughts and behaviors. This is because thoughts, feelings, and behaviors work together in a constant, never-ending cycle. Your thoughts influence your feelings, and your feelings influence your behaviors, which in turn, continue the cycle.

What are Emotions?

Ultimately, emotions are somewhat simple to define in theory. Despite how vastly different they may be from each other; all emotions have some base similarities at their foundation. In particular, they have three key features that define what they are. They are natural, they are reflexive, and they are instinctive.

In being natural, they come on their own. They were created over millennia of evolution and development, forming in ways that would be conducive to the survival of life as life continued to grow more and more complex over time. The more complex and capable of thought life grew, the more emotional capacity was necessary to control them.

Emotions are reflexive, meaning they are reactions to the world around them. If left completely unprovoked with no real stimulus, emotional states do not change much. Things happen around you to sway you into feeling one way or the other. For example, getting hurt can cause negative feelings of sadness, anger, or fear. This is because all three of those emotions can aid in survival in that particular situation—sadness lends itself to getting the support of others. Anger lends itself to defending oneself, and fear lends itself to flee. When emotions are reflexive, they are meant to bolster one's chances at survival.

Lastly, emotions are instinctive. They happen automatically with very little thought involved. They do not require much conscious thought to arise, instead of happening on their own. This is largely believed to be due to the fact that humans have two different thought processes that operate largely independently from each other. Humans have the implicit or automatic thought process, which involves instinctive judgments and behaviors, such as emotions, and they have the explicit or controlled thought process that is responsible for rational thought, learning, and development. Emotions fall into the implicit, unconscious thought process—they occur on their own without feeling the constraints of rationality.

Of course, when they are not constrained by rationality, it is easy to understand how fickle they can be—emotions can largely be influenced by several different external factors. Anything from how the day went to what you ate could sway your emotions.

Why We Have Emotions

Despite how fickle and impractical emotions can be, they have important biological purposes. If they were not important, they would not have developed over the course of several thousands of years in a wide range of species. Many animals with higher brain development have the areas in the brain believed to be responsible for different emotions—it is not solely a human thing. With that in mind, the two biggest purposes for emotions are survival and communication with a crowd.

As briefly touched upon, emotions are reflexive. They are natural, instinctive responses to the world around you meant to boost your survival. This is because they are motivators. Emotions motivate you to perform certain actions and behaviors in hopes of firstly surviving and secondly passing on genes to the next generation. Because you will naturally and instinctively feel certain ways when exposed to certain situations, your own behaviors will be influenced. If something makes you scared, you are likely to approach it cautiously or avoid it altogether. This is because fear serves to put your body on high alert. If something makes you happy, you are likely going to continue to seek exposure to it because happiness is what is felt when needs are met, and means you are doing something right. Of course, this is not always necessarily an accurate way to go about life, but it is a good rule of thumb. Things that trigger happiness, such as love, affection, sex, good food, and rest are all generally good for survival.

Secondarily, emotions serve as a major component for effective communication. When you can communicate effectively, you are better able to survive. You will be able to clearly iterate whatever it is you need in that particular moment simply because emotions are all about your current unconscious thoughts, feelings, and needs revolving whatever is happening around you. Those feelings trigger specific reactions in the body, namely in body language, actions, and expressions, and those three things culminate into a way to nonverbally communicate your needs to those around you. Those who are closest to you are likely to then want to behave in ways that are beneficial to you, actively seeking to meet your needs to ensure you are cared for simply because they understand that you have needs as well. Further, when you can read the needs of others around you, you can also choose to regulate your own behavior. Think of anger, for example—it is largely an alarm emotion. You feel anger when you feel as though you are being wronged or your boundaries have been overstepped. When you feel angry, you will show the typical angry body language. When someone else sees that their own actions have made you angry, they then have the opportunity to tweak their own behaviors to ensure they do not continue to make you feel wronged. Both of these facets of communication aid in the survival of the social species. Because humans naturally crave living in groups of people, surrounded by others, they need to have a good understanding of the thoughts and feelings of those around them in order to live in a happy, healthy manner without angering everyone.

What Emotions Say

We have dozens of emotions—joy may be different than exuberance, for example, and disappointed is different than agony. While they may fall under similar categories of emotions—such as joy and exuberance both falling under the umbrella category of happiness and agony and disappointment both falling, at least in part, under sadness—they are different. Rather than going through each emotion step-by-step to define it, we will look at broader categories. The seven emotions that will be presented here are believed to be the seven fundamental emotions, meaning that all emotions felt will fall under the category of one or several of the emotions listed here. Emotions exist on a spectrum, and they can be quite complex, particularly when you start feeling complicated, conflicting feelings, and for that reason, we will simplify them for the purpose of the book, reducing the wide range of feelings down to the seven universal feelings that are known to occur in all cultures across the world, no matter how distanced or withdrawn the people may be. Each of these seven emotions evokes a specific facial expression in response that can be recognized across cultures. Even people that are born blind and never get to see expressions exhibit the expressions that go along with these seven emotions, making them believed to be universal.

Anger

Anger is felt like a response to something wronging the individual or overstepping a boundary. It is meant to evoke protection or defensive behavior and conveys a deep need for a boundary to be respected or some distance to be given.

Fear

Fear is felt during times of active threat. The individual believes that he or she is in danger, and the body responds to that by preparing to either fight or flee to survive. When seeing this emotion in others, it conveys a need for security and safety.

Contempt

Contempt is felt when an individual feels a deep hatred or disapproval for another person or thing. It is usually caused as a response to not believing in something someone is saying or lacking trust or respect for the other person. It conveys a need for trust.

Disgust

Disgust is usually felt when you are exposed to something that is toxic to your health. It is usually reserved for things that will make you ill if you consume it, but it can also be directed toward people as well if they have done something utterly against your moral code. It usually conveys that whatever is present is toxic and should be avoided at all costs.

Happiness

Happiness is the ultimate sign that you are doing everything right and should continue to do so. It means that the individual is satisfied during that moment and that all needs are met. It is pleasant and meant to encourage the individual to continue doing whatever evoked that happiness response in the first place.

Sadness

Sadness is felt in times of pain or loss. It triggers a withdrawal in which the individual feeling sadness attempts to escape from the cause of the pain or the loss and is a cue that major support is needed in order to heal.

Surprise

Surprise occurs when something startling or unexpected has occurred. It usually means that something that did not line up with prior belief sets has occurred and that it requires further attention in order to understand what has happened.

Chapter 3: Empathy

Another key psychological concept you will need to understand before delving into the mysteries of dark psychology is empathy. This is another one of those traits that is shared across most of humanity, although some people do struggle with it. It is one of those defining features that evolved over time to aid in survival. It is incredibly important to understand because, like emotions, it is highly motivating. This means that if you understand empathy, you may then be able to understand how to sway other people to do what you want, or to manipulate them with your own feelings, knowing that the empath will pick up on them.

Have you ever had a moment in which you looked at another person and understood exactly what they were feeling, no matter how inexplicable the phenomenon may have been? Perhaps you looked at a homeless beggar on a corner and suddenly felt an intense loneliness, pain, and shame just by looking. That is empathy.

What is Empathy?

Empathy allows people to understand the emotions of someone else. Through a glance, when you are an empathetic individual, you can tell exactly what someone else is feeling as though you, yourself, are feeling the same pain. You are able to put yourself in the shoes of the other person, intimately understanding their feelings and recognizing exactly how it impacts them. You can, essentially, understand, recognize, and feel their mental state.

Empathy is a strange ability; it is usually done at a glance, but can also be done by someone sitting in a room with strong emotions. Those who are empathetic are able to pick up on subtle cues, such as the tension in the room or the way people are holding and presenting themselves, and recognize what needs to be done one way or the other. Typically, because they are so willingly able to feel what others are feeling, highly empathetic individuals go above and beyond to help those around them.

Types of Empathy

There are three major types of empathy that show up throughout life, and each serves a slightly different purpose. Ultimately, people are best served with a combination of the three empathies, but being particularly empathetic in all three types is somewhat uncommon. These three types of empathy are emotional empathy, cognitive empathy, and compassionate empathy.

Emotional empathy

Emotional empathy refers to your ability to feel what someone else is feeling. When you see someone exhibiting strong emotions, you are able to read the situation quickly and understand exactly what is being felt by the other person. You may be highly sensitive to the vibes in a room or recognize the tension. No matter how you are able to sense the tension, struggles, and emotions, you often are uncontrollably overwhelmed with the emotion of the other person as if you are in their shoes.

For example, if you are walking down the street and see a young child, scared and sobbing, with no adults around, you may feel your heart panging in fear and sorrow. You understand that the child is likely absolutely terrified and that the parent is also likely absolutely terrified as well, and you feel that same fear. That is emotional empathy. You see and understand the emotions.

Cognitive Empathy

With cognitive empathy, on the other hand, you may be able to look at someone and understand their emotions at a glance, you do not feel them the same way the emotional empath does. You can see the crying child and understand exactly why the child is crying, but you do not feel the same overwhelming feeling of your own fear in response. Instead, you are able to look, rationalize why the child is crying—in this case, because he is lost and young children naturally crave to be with their parents—and being able to remain rational and levelheaded can be quite beneficial. You are able to predict what the child will do next—likely run away screaming, or collapsing on the ground and continuing to sob uncontrollably—and in being able to predict, you can then make sure you are tweaking your own behaviors accordingly. This particular branch of empathy is incredibly important when considering how to influence and persuade other people.

Compassionate Empathy

Separate from the other two empathies, compassionate empathy is a sort of combination of the two. Think of this as the most enlightened of the empathies—it allows for the individual to see someone else and understand intimately what that other person is going through. The compassionate empath sees the pain of the other person and feels it. It adds the layer of cognitive empathy as well—the individual is able to also understand the thoughts of the other party and make predictions based on behaviors when attempting to understand what is happening. Those two empathies combine, and the individual is left feeling a strong desire to help others around him or her. The individual feels motivated in feeling the emotions and understanding the thoughts of the other person. This is the mark of a good leader—it is someone who can see and understand and genuinely want to aid those around him or her.

Purpose of Empathy

Similar to emotions, empathy has one major purpose. It is tasked with ensuring a better chance for the survival of the species. This is accomplished through three separate steps that are integral to empathy as a whole. These three key concepts are communication and bonding, regulation of one's own behaviors, and encouraging selflessness. Each of these three concepts aid in the survival of humanity in different ways.

Communication and bonding

When you are able to recognize and feel the emotions of those around you, you are better equipped to communicate and bond. Think of it this way—if you understand that your neighbor is stressing out over trying to get a fence patched up before the rainstorm that weekend, you can see what your neighbor needs and offer to alleviate some stress. In understanding the other person's unconscious cues and seeing how you can alleviate the discomfort, you are then able to offer a solution, which encourages and facilitates bonding between the two of you. By recognizing when those around you need help and responding in kind, you are able to develop relationships that will serve you well.

Regulation of own behaviors

When you can see how other people understand your own behaviors, you get valuable insight that can be used to regulate yourself. If you see that someone is disinterested in what you are talking about, for example, you see a cue to change the subject to something else or to present what you are discussing in a way that will bring the other person back into the conversation. This can go one step further—if you see that someone is being hurt or upset by your words or actions when you empathize with the other person, you are far more likely to want to stop what you are doing. When you imagine how you would feel with roles reversed, you are more likely to want to stop simply because you understand how you would feel in the same position. Understanding and feeling the other's pain allows you to regulate your own behaviors.

Encouraging selflessness

Lastly, empathy seeks to encourage selflessness. Through the two previous purposes, regulating yourself and communicating, you are more inclined to want to help others. Think about it this way—if you saw your best friend struggling and you had the means to alleviate that suffering, would you do it? Most people would say yes; they would—no one enjoys watching people they love suffer in misery all alone. This serves an extra purpose as well—when you help those around you, they are far more likely to want to return the favor when you need a hand. When people behave selflessly, the entire group is far more likely to survive. For example, if you give your neighbor some food because they are out, your neighbor is much more likely to stop and help you when they see that something has broken and needs patching in order to be functional again.

With these three fundamental purposes of empathy working together, people are more capable of living in relative peace when surrounded by each other. They will want to help each other survive, and in turn will want to continue to help each other survive when everyone is looking out for the best interest of everyone else.

Chapter 4: Principles
of Persuasion

Persuasion is perhaps one of the most innocent ways to control the mind of someone else. In a sense, it qualifies as mind control because it is literally causing someone to shift how they are thinking in line with what the persuader thinks is right. When you are able to master the art of persuading others, you will be able to yield that power when it is necessary, in ways that can be beneficial to both you and those around you that you seek to persuade. Of the different forms of dark psychology, this one is the least insidious. It does not hide and does not attempt to force someone else into doing something. Instead, it is open and honest—advertising its purpose and seeking to encourage those around the individual to do something because they want to rather than out of coercion. The persuader wants everyone to agree with him or her, but not badly enough to force the point or coerce others.

When attempting to persuade someone, there are six principles that should be remembered. Understanding and utilizing these can be incredibly useful when it comes to influencing other people. These six principles are reciprocity, consistency, social proof, likability, authority, and scarcity. Take the next several moments to familiarize yourself with each of these. You will see these concepts come up time and again throughout the rest of the book in a wide range of manipulation and persuasion tactics.

Reciprocity

This is perhaps the most basic of the principles of persuasion—in fact, it is so simple, you have already been introduced to this concept within this book. Reciprocity is the concept of people wanting to give back when they receive. When you help someone, the other person is far more likely to help you. Reciprocity seeks to harness that concept, recognizing it as a truth of humanity, and seeing how useful it can be in encouraging others to do as a persuader desire.

This can be seen even in restaurant settings—when the waiter or waitress brings you a few chocolates or a complimentary treat like a fortune cookie at the end of your meal with your check; you are far more likely to want to give a larger tip than if you had received nothing instead. This explains why so many restaurants do offer up that cheap mint or cookie in response— they want to earn that extra tip.

You can utilize this concept yourself by always making it a point to consider what you can do for other people before seeking the other person to do something for you instead. If you stop and ask what they can do for you, you are not likely to get as far as if you stop and ask what you can do for someone else first. Your mind will be blown the next time you try this. To start, try doing this in a relatively low-stakes environment. Perhaps ask your spouse how you can help one evening, and after the fact, ask your spouse for a favor. Your spouse, if the favor is reasonable, is likely to concede!

Consistency

Consistency is a bit trickier to understand. It is the idea that people make active commitments to the world around them, and they feel obligated to follow through with it. When you have a commitment, you feel the drive to follow through, simply because you want to be considered reliable and committed. While this may not necessarily seem relevant to persuasion, consider this point: If you can get someone to offer a commitment to something, you are more likely to get them to follow through after the fact. People are innately driven to complete whatever they have promised to do so. If you want someone to do something for you, then, you should always seek to get it put into a commitment of sorts in order to ensure it is completed.

With the commitment made, you should then make it known to those around you. Through publicizing the individual's commitment, such as by telling people at work that John over there has agreed to help you with your copying all week, you add an extra layer of pressure to the individual. John is far more likely to try to follow through simply because he wants others to see him as reliable as well. When there are multiple people's thoughts about him on the line, he is far more inclined to push through and complete whatever he has agreed to do so.

Keep in mind, however, that this has to be voluntary. The other person has to want to do whatever it is you are asking them, or they are not going to really feel compelled to follow through with finishing the task. For example, if you attempt to coerce the other person into doing your copying, and they reluctantly agree just to get you off their back, they are not going to feel that same innate drive to finish the work as if they had volunteered to do so on their own.

Social Proof

When is the last time you have walked into a room, looked around, and been entirely unsure what you were supposed to be doing? If you are not sure, think about the last time you went to a busy public building for the first time—you may have been entirely confused as to what you would be expected to do or where you should wait. Instead of standing there without doing anything, you likely looked to the cues of those around you—you appealed to social proof. You wanted to fit in, and so you chose to do what those around you were doing, even though you were still unsure that that was the right thing to do.

People oftentimes rely on the social cues from those around them to understand what they should be doing, thinking, or feeling. Specifically, people want to follow their peers rather than authorities or subordinates.

Understanding this concept can be incredibly important when it comes to persuasion—if you are going to be getting a new group of charges at work, the easiest way to get everyone in line is to get a single person on-board first and allowing everyone else to follow that one particular person's example. You just lessened your own workload and allowed for those around you to be trained quickly and easily.

Likability

Ultimately, people are far more likely to be persuaded when they like the person who is attempting to persuade them. It is a simple fact of life—people naturally reach out to those they know and trust and are more likely to take the advice of someone they trust than someone they do not. This can be used in a wide range of ways, and even if the other person is entirely new to you or does not know you well enough to like you, there are ways you can persuade them to like you so you can then persuade them at a later time.

There are three things that cause people to be more likely to like someone. These are relatability, praising, and being able to cooperate toward a common goal. If you can harness these, you are far more likely to get someone else to like you.

When you are relatable, people are likely to get along better with you. When you can relate to someone, you are better able to empathize, which can allow them to better see that they do like you. The easiest way to make yourself relatable in situations in which you are, for example, a salesperson, is to share a small detail about yourself early on or decorate your room or office with pictures or items that are relevant to you. Maybe you have pictures of your children up, or perhaps you decide to add a photo of yourself engaging in a hobby. Anything goes, so long as it personalizes you.

Secondly, when you want to be likable, you should always make it a point to praise the other person. However, you cannot just make something up or say something that you do not mean— you need to make genuine compliments to the other person. When you lie about praise, you are often seen as doing so manipulatively and, in an attempt, to convince them to want to help out of sheer flattery. Even though you may actually be complimenting them more to get them to agree than out of kindness, you should still make sure that whatever you do say is genuine.

Lastly, you want to make sure you and the other person are working toward the same goal. When you are both working together toward a common goal, the other person is going to be far more likely to want to work with you. Even in situations where you stand to benefit far more than the other person, such as in a sales job when you are trying to sell a car, and you will literally make a commission based off of the cost of the car bought, you should make it clear that you are working toward a common goal. You can do this by pointing out that you want to help the other person, or through phrases such as, "help me help you" that make the other person feel like you are on their side. After all, you are—you want them to get what they want, while also wanting what they want to be mutually beneficial.

Authority

People naturally want to defer to authorities when it comes to certain situations and decision making. This is why people will go get consultations from lawyers or doctors, or they will go to a professional to help with taxes. When someone else is seen to have all of the pertinent information on something simply due to experience or education, it becomes far easier to just defer to whatever that person is thinking or suggesting. By recognizing the authority vested in someone else out of experience and education, people are able to avoid making the wrong decision due to a lack of experience or not knowing how something works. After all, would you want a daycare teacher to decide which surgery you should get to repair an issue? Unless that daycare teacher happened to also be certified as a surgeon, the answer is likely no.

This is incredibly relevant to persuasion—if you can establish yourself as an authority on a topic somehow, people around you will be far more willing and happier to go along with whatever it is that you are requesting of them, which will serve you well. Luckily, there are several ways you can establish authority simply and quickly. The simplest way to do so is through making sure you keep your credentials visible. Place them on your nameplate, or hang your diploma on the wall right behind your desk. You could also make sure that when your clients come in, your secretaries offer some sort of detail that appeals to your authority. If you sell cars, your secretary may say something about how you are the top seller of the month, or if you are a dentist, the receptionist might sing your praises to the person making the appointment. You could also do this yourself by offering small snippets of details about yourself when the client first enters your office, such as making a comment about that one time you were in school at such-and-such prestigious university studying your major. By dropping your credentials subtly and naturally, you set yourself apart as an authority, and you will gain all of the persuasive power and influence with it.

Scarcity

The last of the principles of persuasion is scarcity. This one is also quite simple—it is literally supply and demand. When things are less readily available, people see them as more valuable, and when they are more readily available, they are seen as less valuable simply due to the ease of access. You can introduce scarcity in several different ways depending on the context.

Within a relationship, you may put a time limit on making a serious decision, such as choosing to move in together or give an answer to a proposal. If you are attempting to sell someone something, you can make it clear that the offer that is on the table at that particular moment is limited and will expire shortly. This puts the pressure on the other person to decide quickly.

While putting the limitations on the table, you should also make it a point to show how the other person is likely to lose out if they do not take the offer quickly. By focusing on what will be lost, the other person is more likely to act quickly simply because people do not like the idea of losing out.

Another way to cause scarcity is to make something limited. Think of how restaurants will run limited time only items, such as fancy drinks or menu items. These are only available for a short period of time, and people often fall for the trick, trying to get in to get the limited-time item just so they can say that they have. Especially today, with social media being so influential and people wanting to have everything social-media ready, people are more likely to go out of their way to seek out a rare item just so they can say that they did so.

Chapter 5: Persuasion vs. Manipulation

Many people fail to recognize the nuances between manipulation and persuasion. Despite the fact that both seek to convince someone else to do something else, they are quite different in enough key ways to be classified completely differently. One is only beneficial to the manipulator (manipulation) while the other ideally, should benefit both people. Because of these key differences, manipulation becomes far more insidious than persuasion. The manipulator sees the other person as a tool, a means to an end, whereas the persuader sees the other person as a partner.

Defining Persuasion

Though persuasion involves changing the mind of someone else, it is not necessarily a bad thing—there are plenty of ways that persuasion can be used innocently or benevolently. Persuasion is any method that will actively change the thoughts, emotions, actions, or attitudes of another person toward another person or thing. This change is seen as a persuasion. It can be done inwardly toward oneself through changing one's own attitudes, or it can be done to other people as well.

Usually, persuasion is used as a form of influence—it is everywhere. It is present in ads, politics, schools, professions, and just about everywhere you could think of. If you can think of something, chances are there is some sort of persuasive layer to it somewhere and somehow.

When persuading someone, there are four key elements that must be present. These four elements are:

- Someone who is doing the persuading

- The message or the persuasion

- A target recipient for the persuasion

- A context that the persuasion is received

Each of these four key elements must be present for something to be considered persuasive. Of course, this means that manipulation would fall within the category of persuasion as well.

Defining Manipulation

In psychology, manipulation is a type of influence or persuasion, but unlike regular persuasion, manipulation is covert, deceptive, or underhanded. This means that, unlike regular persuasion, which seeks to be most honest, manipulation is often untrustworthy. The manipulator will have no qualms about lying about the situation or attempting to coerce the target into believing something, so long as he gets what he wants.

The manipulator seeks only to further serve himself—he does not care about the target and does not care about hurting the target. The target is seen as little more than collateral damage—a necessary sacrifice to get the desired results. As such, manipulation tactics are oftentimes quite exploitative and are almost always meant to be insidious and harmful.

Successful manipulation requires three key concepts to happen. These three are:

- Concealing the intentions and behaviors while remaining friendly upfront

- Understanding the ways, the victim or target is vulnerable and using those vulnerabilities to the advantage of the manipulator

- Being ruthless enough to not care about the harm caused to the victim

Manipulation can take several different forms, but most of them follow the pattern of being covert, harmful, and causing no guilt to the manipulator. Several of these methods will be discussed at a later point in the book in various chapters.

Key Differences

Ultimately, persuasion and manipulation are quite similar: They are both forms of social influence, but that is where the similarities end. While persuasion is generally positive, even within dark psychology, manipulation is not. Manipulation is harmful, ruthless, and insidious in every way, shape, and form.

When you are trying to decide whether something is manipulative or persuasive, there are a few questions you can ask yourself to decide. This simple test can allow you to analyze what you are doing and saying to ensure that you are making the choices that work best for you. If you are not looking to manipulate, but the questions tell you that you are erring on the side of manipulation, you know to tone it down a bit, lightening up on the manipulative factors. These questions are:

- What is the intention that has led you to feel the need to convince the other person of something?

- Are you being truthful about your intention and the process?

- How does this benefit the other person?

The persuader is going to be attempting to convince the other person from a good place—they intend to help the other person somehow. While they may benefit too, they are primarily looking out for the other person's best interest. For example, you may try to convince someone to buy a specific car because it will work better for their family than the car that the person is currently looking at. This would be seen as persuasion—you are offering facts about the other car and showing how it would likely serve the person longer and better.

On the other hand, the manipulator is not concerned with the needs of the other person—the manipulator is going to attempt to push for whatever benefits him or her the most. There is no good intention and there will likely not be much truth either. It is also not likely to benefit the other person much or at all, and may even be detrimental to the other person. For example, the manipulator may try to sell a car that is no good for the buyer simply because the other car may be worth more money and therefore net a much higher commission. The car is not likely to be very good for what the buyer needs, but that is not the manipulator's concern. The manipulator would see that as something the buyer should know on his own and not bother pointing out the ways that the buyer may be making a bad decision, even if the manipulator knows the decision was wrong.

Chapter 6: Ethical Persuasion

With persuasion and manipulation so closely related and really only differentiated in a few key ways, you may be wondering how to keep your own persuasion ethical. You may even be wondering why anyone would want to persuade, even ethically. There is a simple reason for this: Persuading others can oftentimes be quite beneficial to the other person, especially when you do so in order to better the other. Think of the best leader you may have ever encountered in your life. Perhaps it was a teacher that just had a way about him that always swayed people to behave. His very presence was enough to keep even the most troublesome students in line, even though those students rarely wanted to actually be in class. He could genuinely keep people involved in class and appeal to everyone, keeping even the students who would largely avoid actually learning in school engaged. He was able to do this through the persuasion of his own. Does this make the teacher a bad person? Not at all—he simply knew how best to deliver his messages to his targets, and in doing so, he was able to persuade those around him to pay attention.

Ethical persuasion can be used in a wide range of situations. It can be used with your own children to keep them behaving well. It can be used at work to defuse stressful situations. It can be used to come to some sort of agreement with a spouse or friend. There are endless possibilities for ethical persuasion if you are willing to give it a chance.

Defining Ethics

Now for the boring part—Ethics. Many people hear the word and feel their brain instantly shut off simply due to the connection to philosophy. However, ethics are important in every context, even if you do not intend to use any of the skills you will be presented within this book.

Ethics, as simply put as possible, are the moral principles that guide everything we do. They are meant to govern the individual's behaviors, ensuring that they are behaving in ways that are beneficial and respectful to those around them. Think of the golden rule you may have learned way back in kindergarten—treat others the way you want to be treated. That is ethics at its simplest.

Importance of Ethics

Despite how boring ethics may be, there is no way to deny that they are important. Think of doctors and lawyers—they have strict codes of ethics that must be followed in order to make sure that proper client-professional relationships are formed. While you may not be a doctor or a lawyer, you should still be striving to live an ethical life simply to feel as though you have not wronged anyone. When you are able to manage ethics, you are able to make sure that those around you have their basic needs met. By behaving ethically, you are ensuring that you are respecting those around you, while also fostering credibility between yourself and others.

When you remain ethical, you are able to better your own relationships with other people. They will see you as a valuable ally and asset—someone who is always mindful of everyone else and not stepping on toes. This is perfect when developing personal relationships as well as developing professional relationships at work.

Ethics can also aid in decision making—since they dictate a specific standard that should be followed, people are able to more quickly create snap-decisions that will be responsible and capable of ensuring that others are cared for. Overall, when maintaining an ethical point of view, you are able to remain professional and reliable.

Remaining Ethical

While it may seem difficult to juggle ethics when attempting to persuade someone else of something, there is a helpful anagram to help you: TARES. This stands for truthfulness, authenticity, respect, equity, and social responsibility. When you keep this in mind while attempting to persuade those around you, you will be better able to keep your own behavior in check. Remember, persuasion, in the right context, can be beneficial to everyone involved. It does not have to be avoided simply because it falls within the same category of social influences as manipulation. If done properly, persuasion is a powerful tool that will enable you to continue to act in an ethical manner while still persuading someone else to do what you see is right.

Truthfulness

When you are testing your persuasion and intent, start first with analyzing the truthfulness of what you are saying. You want to remain truthful and honest when attempting to persuade those around you for good reason—you want the other person to be informed. When remaining ethical, you should recognize the other person as being their own person with their own free will that deserves its own respect, just as you would want for yourself. You would not want someone else infringing upon your own free will, and as such, you should make it a point not to infringe on the free will of others either.

When testing for truthfulness, ask yourself if what you have said is true. Beyond that, though, you must ask yourself if you have omitted any information that you felt would negatively influence the person or keep the person away from acting in the way you would prefer him or her to do so. You must make sure that you are truthful in your communication as well as in your lack of communication—make sure you leave no pertinent information out, regardless of whether the other person has asked about it or not. You want to make sure that the other person is as informed as possible because you want the other person to willingly agree to do what you are asking without coercion and without manipulation.

Authenticity

The next test for ethical persuasion is determining the authenticity of what is being presented. At a glance, this may seem similar to verifying truthfulness, but it goes a little further. In truthfulness, the important part was making sure that everything was accurate and reported wholly and truthfully. With authenticity, you are checking the veracity of the message you are trying to convey. You must ask yourself whether you are doing what you are doing with good intentions. This means that you are not stereotyping, generalizing, or using fear to scare the person into agreement with you.

Ultimately, you must make sure that the message you are conveying is done for good reasons. An easy way to test for this is to ask if you would buy into what is being said if you were presented with just the information on its own. For example, if you are trying to persuade someone to buy a car and you were in that person's situation, such as trying to buy a family car that will fit three car seats, would you take the message that you are presenting as honest, authentic, and trustworthy? If you feel as though you would agree with the reasoning being provided, the message is likely authentic. If you think that you may have a problem with the information presented, you should probably reevaluate the situation and your own behavior and words to make sure you are lining your persuasion up with ethics.

Respect

Next, you want to evaluate to make sure you are acting and persuading with respect. Are you recognizing the individual needs of the person you are attempting to persuade? Is what you are saying something that you would be comfortable announcing to other people as well, or would you be embarrassed or ashamed to be trying to persuade a perfect stranger of the message you are delivering? For example, if you are attempting to persuade someone to buy a minivan, are you appealing to some sort of gender stereotype, or are you genuinely offering up the benefits a van has to offer completely neutrally, such as discussing how spacious the seats are and how nice it is to have doors that slide open instead of swinging open when you are trying to keep track of kids.

If you feel that your message hinges upon something stereotypical in any way, or is not tailored to the individual you are attempting to target with your persuasion, you should probably look into ways you can change the message. You want to make sure that what you are attempting to persuade the other person is not offensive, nor is it done in an offensive manner. You should not, for example, say that the other person must not be educated because they are from a specific minority that has a lower rate of higher education and that because of that, they likely want this one specific car that many lower-educated minorities ask for. That would not be appropriate in this situation—it does not respect the individual as a person and is not respectful in general. Avoid the stereotypes and seek to really get to know and understand the individual you are helping in order to ensure that the information you present is as relevant, respectful, and persuasive as possible.

Equity

The fourth step in analyzing your persuasion, then, is equity. When you are attempting to make sure that your message is equitable, you are seeking to ensure that both you and the other person are on an even playing field. This is incredibly important—you are not looking to lead by coercion or through playing upon the other person's ignorance. You should seek to make sure that when trying to persuade the other person, you are offering up as much information as possible to ensure that he or she feels that an informed decision is possible.

Oftentimes, when people attempt to persuade others, they play off of a lack of information. When someone is misinformed, it is much easier to take advantage of that misinformation. For example, if someone came in for medical treatment and asked for something that was far more expensive and far more than the person actually needed, it would be unethical for the doctor to accept that without ever discussing less invasive options that would be appropriate for treatment. You want to do the same with your persuasion. Back to the example of the car salesperson, if you have someone coming in to trade in his car because he has hit 100,000 miles and the person has always heard that after 100,000 miles, the car is no longer reliable and needs to be replaced. As a salesperson, you may have thought that it would be the perfect opportunity to get in an extra sale, but as the conversation continues, you learn that the person is not in a good place to get a new car, but felt that he had to do so simply because of the mileage, even though everything was working properly. It would be unethical of you not to point out the information that you know would keep the person from buying the car because not pointing that out would simply be taking advantage of his lack of information on the topic. That is not equitable—the other person deserves an even playing field when making decisions, even if giving that information can cause the person to decide against what you are attempting to persuade him to do in the first place.

Social Responsibility

Finally, the last method to check for ethical persuasion is social responsibility. This is when you stop to see if your persuasion is beneficial advice as a whole. If it is not, how can you change how you are persuading to ensure that you are doing so in a way that protects those who may be at a disadvantage? Remember, the point of persuasion is to convince people to do things on their own—it is not intended to be harmful to other people, nor should it be causing others distress.

If your persuasion is generally a good thing and will not have negative implications to the world at large, for example, you are not persuading someone to think of something in a racially biased manner, and it has passed through all of the other steps, then your persuasion method is likely sound and you are free to move forward with it. If it failed anywhere along the way, you are likely going to want to make sure that you are working to make your persuasion methods more ethical. Remember, ethics are respectful. They treat people with basic human decency, something that everyone deserves.

Chapter 7: Manipulators

With all this talk of persuasion and ethics, it is time to get your first real look at the darker side of dark psychology. This chapter will focus on the minds of manipulators, really taking a closer look at the most common traits that manipulators share. Interestingly enough, many manipulators can be predicted simply by having a specific pattern to their behaviors. Despite the fact that they all come from different backgrounds, they often present quite similarly. In this chapter, you will stop and take a look at those common traits manipulators typically exert, you will learn about the dark triad, which is a particularly dangerous triad of behaviors that the worst, most dangerous manipulators possess, and some of the most commonly recognized behaviors of manipulators around you. This chapter is essentially a crash course to recognizing and understanding a manipulator, providing you with all of the basics. Remember, with knowledge comes power, and with that power, you can protect yourself from succumbing to the insidious efforts of the manipulators, who seek nothing more than fulfilling their own selfish interests.

Traits of Manipulators

Manipulators typically follow a playbook, so to speak. They act in certain ways, seek out similar people as targets, and want similar things. These are some of the most common traits of manipulators, as well as examples of each of the behaviors and how each can be beneficial to the manipulator in hurting other people or seeking out what they want. As you read through this, you will begin to recognize all the ways that manipulators, particularly those who hit the dark triad, are missing many of the traits that make us fundamentally human, such as a lack of empathy.

Egotistic

Oftentimes, manipulators are so busy looking at themselves, their achievements, and their goals, that they refuse to acknowledge that those around them may also have goals of their own that they would like to achieve. The manipulator is far more concerned with his own selfish interest than ensuring that those around him will also be satisfied through life, and he will use those around him as a way to boost his own ego in various ways. For example, he may constantly put down a coworker who he sees as less than him simply because it makes his own ego feel better.

Machiavellianism

This is a belief that the ends will justify the means. These people are typically quite manipulative, believing that it is okay to tell people what they want to hear to get the right behaviors and that ultimately the only difference between a criminal and an average person is that the criminal got caught. Those with this trait are often quite charming and charismatic to the untrained eye, but everything they do is manipulative. This is part of the dark triad

Disengaged morally

People who are able to disengage morally do not care about behaving ethically. They do not see those around them as worthy of respect or fair treatment and instead would rather get what they want without regard for the feelings of those around them. They do not care who they hurt or what they have to do—guilt does not occur, no matter what they do. For example, imagine someone who walks down the street and decides to steal a bike that a child left loosely in the yard. The person who is morally disengaged does not care that he has just stolen from a child—it does not matter to him at all. He does not feel bad about the behavior.

Narcissism

Another of the dark triad, narcissists are people who have a narcissistic personality disorder. They typically meet three key criteria: They have delusions of grandeur, constantly have a need to be the center of attention, and lack the ability to feel empathy. Narcissists frequently manipulate other people into either believing their superiority that they believe is inherent, or they manipulate others to inundate them with admiration and attention to keep their egos happy. For example, the narcissist is likely to exaggerate about achievements to make people more likely to admire him.

Entitlement

Oftentimes, those who are manipulators believe that they are superior to others. This entitlement needs no evidence to them—they are happy to assert this as true no matter what, and it is up to the rest of the world to prove them wrong. They believe that they are better than others, and that is used as a justification for the manipulation. Since they are clearly superior, they should obviously be the ones making decisions for the rest of the peons who are clearly unable to think properly for themselves.

Psychopathy

The last part of the dark triad, psychopathy refers to a unique combination of a pervasive lack of empathy and self-control. Psychopaths see no reason to behave in a kind, ethical manner because they do not feel empathy. They see no need to pander to the feelings of others when they do not understand the feelings of others. They are also quite impulsive, oftentimes choosing to act upon behaviors that are dangerous or destructive simply because they can. They will manipulate others to get what they want because they are missing the social cues from empathy that would otherwise keep them from doing so. For example, a psychopath may decide he wants something a family member has and pull all the strings attempting to get it, starting out covertly and ultimately threatening the other person with physical harm if it is not given to him.

Sadism

Those who exhibit sadism enjoy hurting other people. Physical or mental, it does not matter—either is enjoyable for the sadist. These people will manipulate others just for the fun of it, enjoying watching the fallout after the fact. For example, someone who constantly causes problems between friends, telling one friend one thing while telling the other friend the opposite just to cause problems and watch the fallout could be a sadist.

Selfishness

Oftentimes, manipulators are doing so because they desire to increase their own position in the world with no regards to how it will impact those around them. They see other people as little more than rungs on a ladder to climb up, and because of that, they can justify the manipulation. They are willing to lie to someone to make them fail in order to ensure they get a better job or do better in an interview. So long as the lies and manipulation benefit the selfish manipulator in some way, he is happy to do so. The ends justify the means in his book.

Spitefulness

Sometimes, those who are manipulating others do so because they felt the person, they are attempting to manipulate wronged them first. They see the other person as the one at fault and act as such. Even if the manipulation will hurt them in some way or make their situation worse somehow, they are happy to do so simply because they feel that getting back at the other person is worth it. For example, if you have decided to separate from your husband, he may then let the house fall into foreclosure, knowing you cannot pay for it on your own, even though it will absolutely hurt his credit as well. He sees that hit to his own credit and the fact he will lose his home as well as collateral damage.

Dark Triad

As you can see, there are several different traits that a manipulator can take on. However, the most dangerous, insidious combination of manipulative traits is the dark triad. The dark triad involves narcissism, Machiavellianism, and psychopathy. These three traits combined create incredibly dangerous people who have been found to be more likely to commit crimes, create social problems, and are regularly destructive in organizations or companies, especially if they manage to get a leadership role of any kind.

With the dark triad, people typically lack in empathy, compassion, and a willingness to cooperate. You may remember from earlier in this book that all three of those traits are crucial to the survival of the species. People use empathy to communicate and engage in selfless behavior. They engage in compassion to ensure that everyone is taken care of. People use cooperation to foster bonds and make sure that groups like each other while also increasing the chances of survival. Those exhibiting the dark triad are missing the capacity for all of that, making them incredibly dangerous. They are unpredictable to most people, who would never imagine that someone would behave as callously or manipulatively as those who exhibit the dark triad. Because of that, those with the dark triad personality are able to sneak in undetected, suddenly wreak all the havoc they can, and then disappear without a trace, leaving those in his path confused and blindsided to what has happened. If you get involved with someone with the dark triad personality traits, he is likely to be incredibly manipulative with no regard to your own care, and he will be very callous. While he may have seemed great early on, it is little more than an act that is meant to allow him to get into good graces long enough to get what he wants.

Recognizing a Manipulator

Ultimately, understanding the traits of a manipulator can be incredibly beneficial, but understanding those traits does not protect you if you do not know how to recognize the actions of a manipulator. By learning what the biggest red-flag behaviors are, you are more likely to catch on and recognize a manipulator in the act, which leaves you far less vulnerable to their antics and abuse. Manipulators typically share four common characteristics: They are masters at detecting weaknesses in others, they will use those weaknesses they detect against others, they will manipulate others to give something up that works for them, and they will continue to repeat this manipulation until they are stopped, and even then, they will likely continue for a while. When you are trying to identify whether you are dealing with a manipulator, look for these common signs.

Acts of Power

Manipulators always want power. Their desire to find more power is nearly insatiable—they want more and will do whatever it takes to get it. Because they are frequently in positions where they believe they are superior to others, they will repeatedly act out as such, seeking to push other people to obey them in order to prove they are superior. This is an act of power to them—they get what they want through manipulative methods.

Too Good to Be True

Manipulators oftentimes start out seeming perfect. This is for a good reason—if they showed their true colors early on, no one would want to put up with them. For this reason, when they are somewhere new, they will spend the time to set up a good rapport with the vast majority of the people around them. They do this several ways, with the most common being through sweet-talking and love bombing. These tactics will be discussed in depth later, but are important to keep in mind now. In doing both of these, the manipulator will say exactly what those around him want to hear just to butter them up, and those around him will fall for it.

Malignant Humor or Sarcasm

Oftentimes, manipulators love to make jokes that are hurtful, and when called out, they tell the other person that it was only a joke. If you see someone constantly hurting others, laughing it off, and blaming the other person for being too serious, he or she may be a manipulator. This humor is seen as a way to show that the manipulator is superior, inflating his or her own ego while putting down the other person.

Guilt Trips

Oftentimes, manipulators will employ guilt trips as a tactic of choice. This is done in order to guilt the other person into submission, typically done with long sighs and talking about how disappointed they are that they didn't get what they wanted. They may also use behaviors such as the silent treatment or through berating the other person for not being good enough in hopes of the guilt driving the other person to try better. Guilt trips with manipulators sometimes also involve threats of self-harm or suicide, and while they are usually not serious, you should always contact authorities if someone comes to you with intentions of harming themselves or others.

Loud Outbursts

Oftentimes, manipulators turn aggressive when they feel like something did not work out as planned. Because they see themselves as superior and therefore, an authority in their own mind, they expect others to follow suit. When challenged or feeling as though no one is following through with their expectations, they often get loud and aggressive. This is not only a tantrum similar to what a child would do; it also serves to coerce and intimidate the other parties into submission.

Chapter 8: Victims

Just as manipulators frequently share all sorts of similar traits and behaviors, they also share similar taste in victims. Manipulators, like all predators, look for the easiest targets that pose the best chance of success. Just as the pack of wolves will pick off the weakest members of a herd, the manipulator will look for people who they deem are emotionally easy targets, using a sort of natural sense for who to go after. Because they go for these specific traits, they are usually incredibly efficient in what they do. Manipulators have essentially mastered the art of picking up the perfect target. Take a look at some of the most commonly targeted traits, as well as the signs someone around you may be being abused or manipulated.

Traits of a Victim

While some manipulators may go out of their way to target other types of people, the vast majority will go for ease of a target overlooking for a challenge. When they are going to manipulate others, they want to make sure they can get away with it, as well as get away with any of the behaviors they wish to expose the other person too. Some manipulators never move beyond emotional exploitation while others will go out of their way to work their ways up to physical or sexual abuse. Ultimately, these are some of the easily exploitable traits that manipulators everywhere look for.

Empathetic

The perfect manipulation victim is empathetic. When they are empathetic, they are far easier to manipulate. Think back to the reason's manipulators tend to manipulate—one is to get what they want. An empath is going to be quick to tune into whatever it is that the other person needs, and is much more likely to want to give whatever it is, whether it is attention, affection, or companionship. This makes the empath an ideal target.

Further, empaths, especially if they meet some of the other criteria on this list, are frequently quite forgiving. They will be quick to write off some bad behavior as a fluke or an unfortunate consequence of the circumstances, and they will be more likely to believe that the manipulator will not continue the behaviors. They are also more likely to fall for guilt trips, making manipulating them somewhat easier than others. What the empath offers most of all is the patience necessary to put up with the manipulator's antics.

Caregiver

People with caregiver personalities thrive upon taking care of others. They love to make sure those around them have their needs met. They naturally care about what others need and are often also quite empathetic. Because they feel fulfilled taking care of the needs of others, manipulators can typically twist things around to get whatever they want. The manipulator is quite skilled at convincing the caregiver that he needs something he does not, and the caregiver, wanting to make sure the manipulator is cared for, will do so.

Caregivers, in particular, tend to be quite patient—they are willing to put up with far more than necessary simply because they feel they can handle it. They are likely to forego ending a relationship they see as abusive or manipulative if they believe that the cause of that abuse or manipulation is old wounds within the manipulator that are causing the behaviors in the first place. Instead, the caregiver will put up with the manipulation while diligently attempting to fix the manipulator's problems.

Codependent

Codependency and caregiver personalities are incredibly similar—both the codependent and the caregiver will pour themselves into their relationship, hoping to fix the manipulator, but the codependent will wholly identify with the relationship. The codependent is more likely to put up with far worse manipulation and abuse simply because she feels she cannot move on from the manipulator. While she may recognize what is happening, she feels so intricately intertwined with the manipulator and that relationship that she feels there is no life without the manipulator. Her very identity will be wrapped up in caring for the manipulator, catering to his every whim, even to her detriment. Even though it will hurt her, she continues to do so anyway to a fault. Her codependent nature becomes a point of contention for her as the relationship that she feels is all that she is also hurting her. She may not like the way she is being treated, but she will want to continue to pour herself into the relationship.

Grew up in dysfunction

Those who grew up in the throes of dysfunction oftentimes have skewed ideas of what normal is. They see the way they grew up as normal and will oftentimes revert back to what is familiar to them, even if familiar is harmful. For these people, they may see no red flags with the manipulator's behaviors, particularly if manipulation was one of the key features of their own dysfunctional upbringing.

Since they grew up around unhealthy relationships, their own tolerance for abuse is usually quite extreme. They may be annoyed, but see it as unworthy of ending a relationship or friendship. Even things like physical abuse may not be deal-breakers for those who grew up around it and had such abuse normalized for them. This makes them particularly easy targets because they will be so tolerant and already desensitized to much of the abuse and manipulation that the manipulator will be utilizing.

Low self-esteem

Perhaps one of the most attractive of the traits to a manipulator when looking for a victim is low self-esteem. As you will begin to learn as you begin progressing through some of the more technique-heavy portions of this book, you will learn that breaking someone's self-esteem is oftentimes a core theme in much of the manipulation you will be learning about. Manipulators need people with low self-esteem because they will not fight back or make things difficult—instead, they will put up with the abuse and accept whatever is being said simply because they do not have the self-esteem to trust themselves.

Because the first active step in much of the manipulation is usually breaking down self-esteem, manipulators love shortcuts. Just as how a wolf will go for the weakest in a herd, the manipulator will go for the easiest target, and frequently, those are the ones whose self-esteem is already so weak and shattered that they can do whatever they want with impunity.

Ultimately, the more of these traits that an individual has, the more attractive they are to the manipulator. With that in mind, if you feel like you see any of these signs in yourself, these are likely to be your weaknesses. If you know you have low self-esteem, for example, you should be aware of how that can work against you if you are not careful.

Signs of Abuse or Manipulation

Oftentimes, those who have been manipulated show very similar behavioral signs. After being victimized for so long, they pick up similar behavioral patterns in an attempt at self-preservation. Take a look at some of the most commonly exhibited signs and symptoms of manipulation.

Self-Sacrificing or Martyrdom

Those who have been manipulated enough oftentimes develop an attitude that they do not deserve to be taken care of. They see themselves as expendable, not worth the effort it would take to do things for themselves. Rather than focusing on bettering themselves, they focus on making sure the manipulator is cared for, just as the manipulator intended. They will oftentimes give up whatever they are asked to do, or volunteer to be the one missing out simply because they have been conditioned to do so.

Self-Sabotage

Oftentimes, the victim becomes so accustomed to not getting what he or she wants that they will begin to believe they are not deserving of having needs met. They are so used to being seen as expendable and with their needs as unimportant that they will begin to act as such as well. If they get something nice, they will believe that they do not deserve it, which can convince them that they should do something to sabotage what they have. For example, if someone has just gotten a new job that pays well, it is possible that he would decide that he does not deserve that job, and because he does not deserve that job, he would possibly perform poorly unconsciously, believing that he is not good enough anyway, so he has no point to bother trying.

Fiercely Protective of Abuser

People who are regularly exposed to abuse or manipulation frequently become fiercely defensive and protective of anyone they feel threatens them. Because the manipulator frequently convinces the victim that the victim is exceedingly lucky to have someone like the manipulator around, and intentionally manipulates the feelings of the other person in an attempt to trick the other person into falling in love, the victim often feels conflicting emotions when the manipulator is talked poorly about. Oftentimes, the victim will vehemently defend the manipulator to anyone who says something they disagree with, feeling the need to protect the manipulator.

Mental Health Issues

Through constant stress from the manipulator, it is not uncommon by any means for people to develop mental health issues. After extended periods of time being manipulated, belittled, and demeaned in order for the manipulator to gain a sense of control over the individual being manipulated, the victim is more prone to depressive and anxiety symptoms.

Being Distrustful

After time spent being demeaned and manipulated, people tend to grow to be quite distrustful. Especially once they have come to discover the truth and they understand that someone they had trusted actually was using them in some of the worst ways imaginable, they lose the capacity to trust easily and readily.

Fearful Behavior

Because people who are manipulated often find themselves getting to a point where they fear the reaction of the manipulator if they do not concede to whatever the manipulator wants, the victims tend to grow fearful in general. They are so used to someone taking advantage of the situation and making them feel bad about themselves when they are not living up to expectations that they often come to expect the worst from others as well. They grow timid and concerned with assuming that people around them have the worst intentions, and that leads to a fearful demeanor, especially when the victim perceives that he or she has failed in some way.

Paranoia

Typically, in a combination of becoming fearful and distrustful, those who are manipulated sometimes develop a paranoid view of the world. They worry that they are being taken advantage of, even when they are not, and they become inherently suspicious of those who do try to help, assuming there is some sort of ulterior motive at play when someone does offer help. For example, if a manipulation victim is asked if she wants help with studying for an upcoming exam, she may wonder what the other person wants in return, even if the other person is simply doing it out of kindness or a genuine interest in getting to know her better with no strings attached.

Chapter 9: Preventing Victimization

When you are able to recognize manipulators around you, understanding their most frequent behaviors and traits, and recognize that you may have some of the traits that manipulators find attractive, you can prepare to arm yourself against the manipulation through several different tactics. Each of these can help you develop the ability to stand up for yourself, proving to manipulators everywhere that you are not willing to be victimized and not willing to put up with their nonsense. By embracing some of these traits and lifestyles, you will make yourself much less desirable and much less manipulatable, which is usually enough to keep the manipulators at bay. After all, a difficult target puts the manipulator at risk for having his cover blown, something that no manipulator actually wants to see come to fruition.

Understand Your Rights

Perhaps the number one way you can defend yourself from manipulators is to recognize and understand your own human rights. When you are able to recognize your rights and what they are, you are then able to understand when they are being violated. When you are able to recognize when someone else is violating your basic rights, you will be able to stand up for yourself. Just by standing up for yourself and refusing to allow the manipulator the ability to do whatever he or she wants, you are going to deter the manipulator. You make it clear that you are not an easy target simply because you understand what treatment you are entitled to, and you are strong enough to enforce it.

Some of the most basic rights you have as an individual include the following:

- **Right to respect:** Every person deserves to be treated with respect. The catch here is recognizing that there are two fundamentally different ways the word respect can be used—it can mean that you are treating someone with basic human decency, such as recognizing the rights and boundaries of those around you, or it can mean respecting authority, as in listening to what someone who holds authority says you must do. These two types of respect are fundamentally different. You have a right to respect in the sense of being treated with human decency. Remember that the manipulator does not have the right to respect in regards to some perceived authority—he may have the right to human decency, but you do not have to obey what the manipulator says in the name of respect.

- **Right to express yourself:** You are free to have any thoughts, feelings, opinions, and desires you want to have. Of course, you are not free to behave in any way if it violates social norms, laws, or harms another person, but you are more than welcome to decide how you want to feel about a topic without anyone else having room to criticize your decisions. Remember this—oftentimes, manipulators like to try to strip individuals of their ability to think for themselves.

- **Right to autonomy:** Especially once you have reached the age of majority, you are free to be your own person. You are welcome to choose what you decide to make a priority as well as what you are choosing to consider a waste of your time. No one can tell you how you should spend your time without your consent, and if you are willing to stand up for your freedom of having your own thoughts and autonomy, the manipulator is going to get bored very quickly. If you are not open to his tactics, he will not waste his time when there are other people who will fall for his tricks much more easily without risking exposing himself.

- **Right to say no:** By and large, there is very little that you are actually required to do by law. Beyond paying taxes and ensuring that you are not infringing on the rights of anyone else, you are mostly free to do or decline to do, what you want. You are more than welcome to tell the manipulator no, and you should be free to do this without feeling any guilt about doing so.

- **Right to take care of yourself:** You should never be made to feel bad for taking care of yourself—ultimately, the only person who is likely to take care of you the way you will need is yourself, and if you cannot count on yourself to do so, you are going to find yourself and your health, both physically and mentally, suffering. This also means that you are free to protect yourself from toxic individuals—even if the manipulator is your mother, your sibling, your spouse, or even your child, you are well within your rights to stand up for yourself, even if that ultimately means that you cut off the other person if they refuse to respect your boundaries.

- **Right to happiness and a healthy life:** Remember, everyone deserves happiness, and everyone deserves to be able to live a physically and emotionally healthy life. You have the right to this, and to creating your own happiness through all of the above. Even if the manipulator attempts to convince you that you do not deserve happiness for any reason, remind yourself that you do and refuse to let the manipulator put that thought in your head.

While most people will respect these rights without too much fuss, giving you the freedom and respecting your boundaries accordingly, there are people out there who would love nothing more than to steamroll over every individual right, depriving you of all of them in order to control you. Even if the manipulator tries to take advantage of you, remember one key fact: There are only strings involved if you let them be involved. You have all the power here—your own autonomy is your greatest asset, and if you refuse to surrender it, you will be able to protect yourself.

Stay Away from Known Manipulators

Another easy way to protect yourself is through sheer distance. If you automatically take some distance from the other person because you have a feeling that what he is doing may or may not be manipulative, you will protect yourself. Manipulators require proximity, both personally and physically, to really be able to work their magic, and if you decline to give them that power, they will not be able to take control over your life.

Distance will also allow you to identify whether someone is actually the manipulator you may suspect him or her to be— with distance, you will be far more likely to be able to see whether or not the other person actually is a manipulator. From a distance, you can study the other person's behaviors when interacting with other people. You may be able to see the mood swings, such as shifting from being aggressive with one person, but playing the victim with another, if you are on the sidelines, avoiding detection.

Avoid Taking Things Manipulators Say to Heart

Remember, the manipulator wants nothing more than to break you down and exploit any vulnerabilities or weakness he or she may see within you. When they are able to recognize a weakness, manipulators often attack it with as much power as they can muster in order to break you down. Despite how difficult you may think protecting yourself will be, you have one key skill that will protect you—refuse to personalize.

Personalization is the idea that you take the blame for everything that is happening around you. If the manipulator is in a bad mood, you may naturally assume it was something you did, especially if the manipulator has taught you to have such a reaction. However, when you stop taking things personally, you are able to begin distancing yourself from the emotional reactions that the manipulator wants you to feel. He ultimately wants you to feel like it is your fault because guilt is something that can be easily exploited, and when he is able to exploit you through your guilt, you are going to be more within his control.

Along those same lines, recognize that you are not at fault here. It is not your fault that the manipulator chose to target you or attempt to target you, and you should not allow yourself to feel guilty for the actions of the other party.

Shift the Pressure onto The Manipulator

Oftentimes, those who are manipulative are far more willing to put unreasonable or unfair pressure onto their victims. They will demand things of you that would make most people balk, but nevertheless, the manipulator continues with his demands.

They oftentimes will repeat these demands, growing aggressive in order to intimidate you into obeying. Luckily, there is one simple way that can usually take the wind right out of the manipulator's sails: Shift the pressure back.

If the manipulator asserts that you must go and run to three different stores to get the food for dinner that night because he has to have the tomatoes from store A, the cheese they offer in the deli at store B, and the specific cut of meat at store C, for example, you could stop and point out the inequity. The easiest way to do this is to ask deflecting questions that shift the pressure back onto the manipulator. A few examples of these questions include:

- "Is that really reasonable to you?"
- "Would you go out of your way to do all of this without complaint?"
- "Is this a request or an order?"
- "How does this benefit me?"
- "What about my opinion?"
- "Does this sound fair?"
- "Are you seriously expecting me to do xyz thing?"

These questions put the manipulator in a tough place—he can either say that yes, he does think what he is asking is fair, in which case he opens himself up to you requesting that he goes to do it if it is fair and reasonable, or he has to admit that no, it is not fair or reasonable to demand you to go and do whatever he has decided he wants.

While this method will work with several different kinds of manipulators, it does not work for everyone. Certain types of manipulators, especially those with the traits of the dark triad, may decide to completely ignore your attempts to prove their actions unjust and unfair.

Take Advantage of Time

When manipulators make demands, both reasonable and unreasonable, they regularly enforce some sort of time limit. Manipulators want their answers immediately because when people make instantaneous decisions without having the time to think them over, they are far more likely to make decisions that are not conducive to rationality or fairness. When people make snap decisions, their emotions are likely making the decisions for them, and emotions are far more easily controlled than rationality. Think about how salespeople will utilize this— they say that there is a limited time on that offer, and if you do not act upon the deal instantaneously, you are not going to get the deal whatsoever. Manipulators will use similar concepts to pressure people into giving them an instant answer.

When you are faced with such pressure, the best thing for you to do is assert that you will consider it. You can tell the manipulator that you will think about what he or she has said, giving it the consideration that it deserves, and asserting the power you truly have within the situation. Ultimately, the manipulator cannot manipulate you if you refuse to give him the ability to do so, which is something you can do quickly and easily if you choose to do so.

Learn How to Say No

When you learn the skills necessary to say no and mean it without imploding a situation, you are more likely to deter manipulators. When you can forcefully put your foot down, you are able to then make it, so the other person has no choice but to accept your no or look irrational and unreasonable by forcing the point further after hearing you already say no. Some tips when it comes to asserting yourself include:

- **Be clear**: Just say the word no. Do not try to weakly imply your intention and outright tell the person that you are not okay with whatever the other person wants.

- **Be assertive**, yet polite: There is a fine line between assertive and aggressive, and that line is typically politeness.

- **Be firm**: Do not give the other person any room to negotiate if the issue is non-negotiable. If the other person cannot accept your no, there is a problem there—and it is not with your decision to say no.

- **Be selfish**: No one else is going to take care of you, so ultimately, you must make it a point to care for yourself when no one else will. Remember this—you must say no in order to better yourself and your situation sometimes, and that is okay.

Set Boundaries and Enforce Consequences

Manipulators love to steamroll over boundaries. They do not care to respect what other people are asking for and instead prefer to act in ways that work for them. The manipulator only wants to ensure that he is cared for, without regard for what you or any other victim feels. You can try to mitigate this by enforcing boundaries. This has two key components:

- Asserting the boundary
- Enforcing the boundary

When you assert your boundary, you allow the other person to see exactly what you are expecting and how you expect things to play out. The trick here is for you to be very firm in whatever boundary you set. You should not be willing to give an inch when it comes to enforcing your boundaries. They are not things to be compromised over, and if someone violates whatever boundaries you have, you should enforce a consequence of sorts for doing so. For example, if a manipulator continues to call you names after you have asked him to stop, you should follow through with whatever you threaten to do in response, such as disengaging from the conversation altogether or choosing to walk away from the manipulator and taking a time out from the relationship.

Chapter 10: Nonverbal Communication

While understanding the words someone says is always essential when attempting to understand what is going on in their minds, words are easily corrupted and manipulated. They can be falsified relatively easily and twisted into lies and other forms of denying what is actually happening or what the other person actually means. Luckily, however, humans have evolved to communicate plenty through nonverbal cues. If you can master these cues, learning how to read body language, expressions, and proxemics, you will be better able to understand exactly what is happening on the inside of the mind of those around you. This is one of the easiest ways to mind read, and while there is a lot to learn, reading people's body language is largely pretty simple when you know what to look for.

What is Nonverbal Communication?

Nonverbal communication refers to several different ways humans communicate without saying a word. Have you ever looked at someone and knew by the way their shoulders hunched over and their expression that they were extremely uncomfortable with whatever situation was happening around them? You recognize that discomfort simply at a glance due to your ability to read their body language.

Ultimately, there are several different forms of nonverbal communication, all of which being beneficial when you are wanting to understand the truth behind what the other person is thinking or feeling. The forms of nonverbal communication that this chapter will focus on includes facial expressions, body language, proxemics, and touch. While there are others, many of the other forms, such as hand gestures, are much more contingent upon culture. If you are interested in learning more about reading gestures, however, you should absolutely look up a local guide to hand gestures in your country of origin.

Expressions

Expressions refer to the wide range of ways that faces move in order to express emotion. They are used to convey emotions most of the time, but they can also be used to show when someone is uncomfortable, lying, or even just not paying attention. Here are some of the most common facial expressions, as well as what some of the most common body language of the face implies.

Universal Facial Expressions

The universal facial expressions are a set of seven different expressions that people can understand and read, regardless of culture or how much or little they are raised with others. Even those who are born blind will still show these facial expressions without having ever seen them before, leading psychologists to believe that these expressions absolutely are innate in human beings as a whole. These expressions are usually sorted out by the emotion they represent.

- **Surprise:** When someone is exhibiting surprise, they usually raise their eyebrows, with the centers raising higher than the edges, creating a rounded look, and also pushing up skin onto the forehead, creating wrinkles. The eyes are wide, with whites being flashed both above and below the iris. Oftentimes, the mouth is opened loosely and without tension.

- **Fear:** When afraid, people usually raise their eyebrow, but instead of them being rounded, they are instead relatively straight. The individual who is afraid will also show a wrinkled forehead in the center, typically between the eyebrows. They also usually show widened eyes, but the whites of the eye are seen from the top part of the eye and not the bottom. The mouth may be open slightly, with lips parted and pulled back with some tenseness.

- **Disgust:** When someone looks at something in disgust, usually the eyelids are raised up with the brows dropped lower. The nose is usually wrinkled while paired with a raised upper lip. The wrinkling of the nose usually causes lines underneath the eyes, at the top part of the cheek.

- **Anger:** Anger is quite easily recognized at a glance. When someone is angry, their brows are lowered and knitted together, creating wrinkles between the brows running vertically. The eyes stare harshly, with the lids tensed. The lips will be either sealed shut firmly, frowning, or wide open if yelling.

- **Happiness:** When genuinely happy, people usually smile. Their lips pull upward, and they sometimes flash their teeth while smiling. There is usually a discernable line running from the nose to the corners of the lips, and there should be creases around the eyes when genuinely happy.

- **Sadness:** When people feel sad, their eyebrows draw together, with the inner corners raising upwards, creating wrinkles between them. The lips are pulled downward in a frown, and the jaw is raised upwards. Oftentimes the lip is pushed outward in a pout.

- **Contempt:** Contempt is largely characterized by a neutral expression with the corner of the mouth raised on one side and a hard stare.

Eyes

The eyes have several different forms of nonverbal communication—from where they look to how they move, plenty can be told about someone's inner thoughts by paying special attention to the eyes.

- **Eye contact:** When people intentionally make eye contact, pay attention to how it is regulated. If the person avoids eye contact, they likely want to end an interaction or avoid an interaction due to insecurity, disinterest, submission, or even deceit. Conversely, making eye contact with others shows interest, and when it is forced and held in a hard manner, it implies dominance and aggression.

- **Frequency of blinking:** People blink at different rates depending on whether they are honest or not. Those who are blinking more than normal are usually under some sort of stress, perhaps due to attempting to figure out how to navigate a difficult situation, or possibly due to trying to come up with a convincing lie to sell to other people. Those who blink less are seen as aggressive or dominant.

- **Pupil dilation:** Though far more difficult to recognize at a glance, especially if the other person has dark eyes, pupil dilation tells a lot about a person. Someone with dilated pupils is either attracted to the person he or she is talking with or lost in some pretty intensive thought.

- **Direction of gaze:** People regularly look at what they are interested in. If you notice someone is repeatedly glancing away from you, whether at an exit or at another person, it is a cue that the other person wants to leave and go interact with whatever keeps drawing his or her gaze. It can also be used to tell which side of the brain is actively working—when people look to the left, they are recalling truthful information while those who are looking to the right are typically using the creative parts of their brains that are responsible for telling lies.

Mouth

People oftentimes may be so focused on censoring the words that come out of their mouths that they forget that they must also pay attention to how the mouth moves. People's mouths are awfully telling in terms of how they are moving.

- **Relaxed lips:** When someone is sitting with relaxed lips, they are usually feeling confident and comfortable in their situation.

- **Parted lips:** People part their lips for several reasons. Most commonly, they are attracted to the person they are interacting with, or they are trying to get a word in or to catch the attention of another person.

- **Baring teeth:** This is either good or bad with no in-between—the individual is either smiling, which conveys positive emotions, or snarling, which is conveying anger or aggression.

- **Twitching lips:** Lips can twitch for several reasons ranging from feeling contempt to trying to hide something.

- **Biting lip or cheek:** Oftentimes, people may chew on their lip or cheek when they are feeling nervous. They are attempting to self-soothe through this action. It can also convey deception, however, such as if the person is trying to censor his speech.

- **Touching mouth with hand:** This is another sign that can have several meanings—it could imply that the other person is stressed out and self-soothing, just like when biting the lip or cheek, or it could be a sign of deception or feeling distrustful toward the other party.

Eyebrows

Just like the mouth and eyes, the eyebrows are incredibly telling about what someone else is thinking. Take a look at these common forms of nonverbal communication involving the eyebrows:

- **Lowered brows:** When someone exhibits lowered brows, he may be showing signs of wanting to hide or retreat, especially if the person is lowering the head. This can also be a sign of deception, in which the individual is attempting to hide.

- **Raised brows:** When someone raises their eyebrows, they signify that they are feeling surprised, or is used to emphasize something that is being said. It may also be used to show attraction to the other person, or sometimes, even submission.

- **Single brow raised:** One brow raised usually comes along with the connotation of disbelief or cynicism.

- **Knitted brows:** This is when the individual pulls the brows together, creating creases in the gap between the brows. It usually shows sadness or confusion.

- **Middle of brows raised:** When the middle of the brows arch upwards, it shows surprise, anxiety, or relief, depending on the context and other parts of the expressions.

- **Middle of brows lowered:** When the middle of the brow is lowered, creating a straight line instead of curving, it usually conveys frustration of some sort.

Body Language

Beyond expressions, people's bodies are actually quite expressive. Just because the hands do not have eyes and a mouth does not mean that you cannot look at the hands of someone else and recognize what they might be feeling. This section will take you from the head down, looking at various types of body language in order to create a comprehensive guide for you.

Head

The head can express so much more than what is plastered on the face. Take a look at some of these ways people communicate without words without the face.

- **Head tilt:** You know what this is—it is the look that a puppy gives you when you say something that it does not understand. When humans tilt their heads, it is for slightly different reasons. Oftentimes, people tilt their heads toward an individual with whom they have rapport, or if they assume that that particular person has authority. When someone tilts their head away, it usually means that the individual is unsure and suspicious of the situation as a whole. When the head is tilted to the side, it can show interest in continuing to listen.

- **Nod:** The nod is the sign of affirmation. It tells the other person that you are listening, even if you are not looking at the speaker at that moment. It identifies that the individual is actively listening to the other party. Pay attention to the speed at which people nod—doing so quickly typically implies that someone is waiting for you to wrap up speaking whereas slower, patient nodding is typically a good thing, implying that the other person feels patient and willing to continue listening.

- **Position of the chin:** The chin can also be quite telling, surprisingly enough. When the chin is raised up, flashing the neck, it shows arrogance or authority. When it is tucked in, however, it implies sadness and insecurity.

Arms

Arms can be used to do a wide variety of different things in order to convey what an individual is feeling. Take a look at some of these common ways to hold the arms when communicating nonverbally.

- **Crossed arms:** This often conveys defensiveness in some way. It is typically done when the individual wants to protect or guard himself. If the individual has arms crossed with thumbs up, it implies that the individual feels confident in the situation, but still feels the need to be defensive just in case.

- **Still arms:** When the arms are completely still, resting neutrally on either side, or one arm is reached across the body to still the other arm, it implies deception. The individual is physically attempting to control his behavior.

- **Arms pulled back:** When the arms and shoulders are pulled back, the individual is conveying a feeling of defensiveness. With the arms pulled out of reach, the individual is making himself less vulnerable to an attack.

- **Arms raised up:** Oftentimes, people raise their arms upward in some sort of exaggeration, regardless of whether it is exaggerating joy, anger, or even confusion. Pay attention to other body language to get a better read on this.

- **Arms expanded:** When the arms are expanded outward, or drawn inward, you can tell the mood. When the arms are expanded outward, they are usually far more relaxed, whereas drawing inward usually conveys stress or tenseness.

Hands

Hands can be quite difficult to track simply because there are so many different positions they can make. Here are the most common nonverbal communications through the hand's body language.

- **Hands behind back:** This implies confidence—the individual is making himself entirely vulnerable with hands hidden behind him. It exudes confidence and authority.

- **Hands-on hips:** Typically misconstrued as aggressive, but is actually used to show someone is at the ready. You see this pose often with people that must show that they are an authority figure in some way to show assertiveness.

- **Hands in pockets:** This shows that the individual is reluctant or distrusting toward the situation or people around him or her.

- **Rubbing hands:** Rubbing the hands together often shows an eagerness or anticipation for what is about to come.

- **Fists clenched:** When someone's fists are clenched, they come across as firm and stubborn. They show that they will not back down, and may also be aggressive.

- **Pointing:** Pointing is used authoritatively. It shows disapproval or anger when done by a superior to someone else, and if it is done peer-to-peer, it is quite confrontational.

- **Clasping hands together:** When hands are clasped together, the individual is oftentimes attempting to self-soothe. They may be anywhere on the spectrum from uncomfortable to terrified.

- **Steepling:** Steepling is when the hands are put into a praying position, but the only contact between the hands happens at the pads of the fingers. The hands are held parallel from each other without contact. This conveys confidence or power.

- **Palms downward:** When palms are held downwards with a hand that is outstretched, it usually shows that the speaker is trying to be dominant and to show authority and that the individual will not be changing their perception of something.

- **Palms upward:** When palms are held upwards, the individual is conveying acceptance and trustworthiness.

- **Hands-on heart:** Hands-on the heart involves a desire to be seen as being honest or speaking from the heart. However, this is easily falsified and should be taken with a grain of salt.

Feet and legs

The legs and feet also show plenty about what a person wants, and these are far less frequently censored. People do not think their bottom half is nearly as expressive as it actually is.

- **Feet pointing away from speaker:** When someone's feet and legs are pointed in a direction that is not the person speaking with him or her, the individual is conveying that the conversation is not wanted. They may have lost interest or feel uncomfortable with the interaction.

- **Feet pointing in the direction of the speaker:** When people's feet point in the direction of the speaker, however, it conveys that the individual is actively interested in what the speaker is saying. It also shows that the listener trusts the speaker.

- **Toes pointed upward:** Sometimes, people will sort of roll on their heels, pointing their toes upward. This is usually showing contentment, especially when paired with smiling.

- **Bouncing on feet:** Some people will bounce on their feet somewhat, similarly to how children do. This shows excitement or nervousness, and the individual is attempting to rid his or her body of excess tension.

Proxemics

Oftentimes, people will alter how closely or far apart they stand to another person. It can happen entirely unconsciously, and you may even begin to notice it in other people—For example, if you are on a date, you may notice one person subtly lean inwards if he or she is interested in the other person, and if something happens that causes some sort of bump, the person may lean out again, creating a distance between each other. This can be incredibly telling as you go about interacting with other people in various ways.

Close

As a general rule, the closer together people are to each other physically, the more likely they are to have a closer personal relationship. When people trust each other, they have what is referred to as rapport with each other—this is essentially a measure of the relationship. People with more rapport are seen as more trustworthy, whereas someone who has not developed much rapport with a certain crowd may not be acknowledged or welcomed nearly as much. People will lean inward toward those they develop rapport.

Far Apart

If people seek to be closer together when the relationship is good, you can then imagine that they are likely to separate themselves out and seek distance if the relationship is poor. Those in a bad relationship with someone, or who do not trust someone, are more inclined to seek a natural distance between themselves and the other party. After all, what good would it do anyone to hang around someone you do not trust? Likely not much. If the other person is actively creating space between himself and you, do both of you a favor and end the conversation.

Touch

The way you touch someone can also convey an awful lot about your mood in ways you may not have ever even considered. When an individual is more open with the touch, allowing full contact between the palm and the other person's skin, it implies comfort and familiarity. Someone would not be that direct with someone they do not know or trust. Conversely, if the individual touches with only the fingertips, it shows that the individual is far more distanced, and perhaps even uncomfortable with the situation.

Likewise, the temperature of the touch can also be quite telling. When the touch is warmer, it shows that the individual is far more comfortable with what is going on, and when the touch is colder, it shows that the individual is stressed or tense and is feeling the effects of anxiety through the fight or flight response, which redirects blood flow, and therefore warmth, to the core.

Chapter 11: Falsifying Nonverbal Communication

Sometimes, you may be in a position where you have to falsify body language. Perhaps you want to fool someone into believing something, or you simply want to come across as something other than what you are or what you are actively feeling. This can be beneficial in several careers where you must be seen as confident and in control, such as with doctors, lawyers, and politicians. With your understanding of how your body language can influence others, of course, you may feel the urge to falsify it sometimes—it can literally benefit you to do so. Here is a list of some of the ways to control your body language and ensure that it works in a way the benefits you rather than works to your detriment.

Power Poses

Before you find yourself in a situation when you have to begin falsifying your information, and if time allows, you should start by spending some time in a power pose. While these may feel ridiculous at first, they are fantastic at soothing the nerves of those who use them and granting them the confidence and power they will need in order to ensure that they can navigate through difficult situations smoothly and effectively.

Even if you are already actively nervous before starting, you will find your nervous energy melting away if you remember these poses. Start by standing up straight, with your feet apart. Hold your head up high and place your hands on your hips, with your chin jutted outward. Stay in this position for two minutes, and you will begin to feel its effects almost instantly. You will find yourself growing more confident and feeling more able to deal with other people, no matter how stressed you were just prior to engaging in the pose. While this may seem unnecessary, it will provide confidence that can help you if you are too nervous about moving forward with falsifying body language.

Smile

When in doubt, most of the time, you can get away with a smile. Especially if you are doing something that is already difficult, by smiling, you are fooling not only the other person to whom you smiled but also your brain. If you can engage in smiling, you can self-regulate, cueing to your brain that you are okay and that there is no reason to come across as stressed out. This then allows you to convince the other person of whatever it is that you are feeling in that moment. You can also make the other person feel more confident in the interaction with well-timed smiles scattered across the interaction.

Angle Your Body

Ultimately, standing face-to-face can come across as incredibly confrontational, and for a good reason—people do tend to get up close and personal when they are engaging in aggressive behaviors. Especially if you can tell that you are angry, but you want to come across as more in control and level headed to get the results you want, you can try angling your body slightly. If you are able to shift your position, even just slightly, to ensure you are standing at an angle, you will not come across as nearly as aggressive.

This pose can also be used if someone else comes at you confrontationally, but you wish to remain in control without the situation escalating. You can shift just slightly, creating a small angle with your body, and maintaining eye contact as you do so. You will come across as in control of the situation, but as if you are not interested in a challenge or confrontation.

Use Your Hands—But Not Too Much

When you are trying to convince people to believe your body language, try using your hands more. When you add in gestures to punctuate your language, you are able to come across as more confident and in control. This has an added bonus of also encouraging the body to fall into the flow of your speaking easier, allowing you to perform better as well.

However, it is also important to know when your body language is too much—if you begin gesturing with your hands above your head, for example, you will come across as more out of control than if you keep your hands constantly below the shoulder line. Raising your arms can look silly, or even aggressive, depending on the movements you are attempting to make.

Make sure you are familiar with the hand gestures local to you before you begin utilizing them—many are contingent upon location and culture, and some of the signals you may use in one country that are positive could be entirely negative in another.

Props

When you are worried about someone seeing the ways, you are attempting to alter your body language, you can introduce props. This can be things like a drink or a cup of water, especially if you want to hide your own negative body language. For example, if you know that you are nervous or uncomfortable in a situation, but you do not want to be sitting with your arms crossed the entire time, you can try holding onto a drink. You still maintain the comfort of having something between yourself and the other person, but you no longer would come across as quite as closed off as before.

These props can also distract from your truer intentions, drawing attention if you bring something a little less conventional. For example, if you are going to be leading a presentation, but you are nervous or uncomfortable, by bringing something to show off, perhaps a souvenir from a recent vacation, you can distract others with the exciting new object, making them less likely to notice your own attempts at altering your own body language.

High Energy

One of the ways people are quickly caught in falsifying their behaviors is due to energy level. People may show the wrong kind of energy, such as appearing to be too tense and nervous, and that betrays their actual feelings and body language. No matter how much you may have mastered controlling your body, if your energy level is incongruent, you are going to be noticed.

Oftentimes, the mistake people make is going into situations without high enough energy levels. Especially if they are already feeling out of their element, they may show low energy, or an unnatural stillness, both of which can ring those alarm bells in the minds of those around them.

Attention to Eye Contact

The number-one place people tend to overcorrect is with eye contact. When you force it, you realize that you are holding it painfully long while making it unconvincing. When you do not make eye contact, people tend to think you are lying, even if you are only redirecting your eyes out of your own discomfort or anxiety. In order to be seen as really confident, you should try mastering the art of eye contact and knowing when and how much is appropriate.

There are ways for you to make your eye contact seem more natural, or to feign eye contact altogether if it makes you uncomfortable. For example, you can try shifting from eye to eye when making eye contact, shifting the eyes when natural. If you are worried about staring for too long, you can try glancing away every 5 seconds or so for a split second, and then making eye contact again, switching the eyes.

If you struggle with eye contact in general, you can also usually fool people into thinking you are making eye contact with them by looking at their nose, right in between their eyes. They often will assume you are making eye contact, but those who are actively paying more attention may catch onto what you are doing and think you are being underhanded or manipulative.

When you do feel the need to break the gaze with the other person, make sure you are looking to the side rather than down as well—when you look down, you seem to be showing submission or even shame, which may cue to the other person that you are lying. Instead, glance to the left, which shows that you are being truthful.

Chapter 12: Using Body Language to Influence

From the previous sections, which all focused solely on body language, you may be feeling pretty confident about understanding how important good body language really is. From here, the natural progression is beginning to use your own body language to influence others into believing or trusting you. This, of course, is quite important—whether you are influencing others around you, persuading them into believing or doing something, or even wanting to manipulate others, you need to be seen as trustworthy. Luckily, establishing yourself as confident and trustworthy is actually quite easy once you have learned the ins and outs of doing so. Take a look at these seven steps for influencing others to believe you. If you do this, you will be seen as more trustworthy, which will make you far more competent when it comes to persuading someone to do something for you.

Smile

At the beginning of your first interaction with someone, you should always smile. Though this may seem silly, smiling is incredibly powerful and conveys a lot about who you are. When you smile immediately after approaching someone when you acknowledge each other, you are seen as warm and approachable in general. People feel deterred and unconfident when they walk up to someone else, and the other person stares back blankly—they feel as though they are unwanted and that they should go off to find something else to do. People do not want negative interactions, and by not smiling when someone first approaches you, you are giving them the cue that things will be negative.

Remember, it is important for these smiles to be genuine in order for the person to really believe you. Fake smiles are one of the easiest things to identify in interaction with other people, so make sure yours are real. If you are in a bad mood or cannot think of a reason to smile at that moment, try thinking back to a memory that always makes you smile, or a silly joke, or something you are looking forward to. It does not even have to be related to the person who you are approaching—the important part is to smile.

Mirroring

This skill is so incredibly important when it comes to influence and persuasion that it will get its own chapter here shortly. However, the gist of mirroring is that when someone trusts you, they naturally mimic your movements. You can take advantage of this knowledge—by mirroring the other person's behaviors, you tell the other person's subconscious that you trust them, which makes them more willing to open up and work with you. They are far more likely to want to like you if they think you like them. Keep this in mind as you are interacting with someone and want to influence them—you are far more likely to gain that influence if they think you like them.

Nodding

If you want someone to tell you yes to something, you can usually sway them to do so with subtle nodding. Of course, you want to do this in a way that is not obvious. Keep mirroring in mind—people want to mimic what someone they have a rapport with is doing simply out of instinct alone. You are attempting to convince someone else to say yes by starting the subtlest nods you can manage prior to asking the question and continuing to do so as you ask. They are likely to start nodding as well as they watch you, and when they are already nodding, their first instinct is going to be to say yes to the other person, whether it is something they would have interest in doing or not. The trick here is to get the other person into the mindset of wanting to do something by appealing to the fact that they will want to follow along with your own emotions.

Standing

Particularly when you are attempting to exert any sort of authority or dominance over someone, the easiest way to do so is to make yourself seem taller. You could stand up while talking to someone while they sit, for example. When you are doing this, the other person naturally feels that you have more dominance than they do simply because you are perceived as bigger than them.

However, as you do this, you need to make it a point not to lean over the other person. When you are leaning over them, or standing over them, you can come across as intimidating to the point that you will be ruining the confidence effect that you were trying to impose. If someone is intimidated by you, your confidence is not what they are focusing on—they will be focusing on your aggressive or intimidating behaviors instead.

You can also use standing up to bolster your own confidence, similarly to how you could stand in the superman pose—if you do when on a phone call, for example, you are more likely to feel confident and able to function effectively. When you feel confident, you can better assert yourself, and when you can better assert yourself, you are more likely to get the results you want.

Leaning

While you do not want to lean over someone, when you are able to lean yourself, you are able to convince the other person that you are more interested in the conversation. For example, if you tilt your head just slightly, the other person perceives it as interest. You can further this effect by leaning inwards during a conversation, particularly if you are both seated across from each other. When you lean inward a bit, the other person feels as though you are really listening to them, and that feeling of validation is oftentimes enough to sway the other person somewhat into feeling like they should be more agreeable.

However, remember you should never lean in too closely, or the other person is going to struggle to trust you. Leaning in too much can make the other person feel that you are threatening them and that can completely ruin your attempts to influence the other person. It is okay if the other person leans back slightly, depending on the context, because doing so implies that they are acknowledging that you are in control of the situation. Knowing exactly how much to lean inwards without intimidating or threatening others is a crucial skill to learn, and it is one of those things that requires practice to discover.

Use Your Feet

Remember how telling the feet are—if you understand that they can be used to acknowledge what someone is interested in, you can use this to your advantage. By using your feet to point toward something or someone, you show that person that you are interested in him or her, and that can help you build trust. With trust comes to influence, and with influence comes the power to persuade.

You can use this further as well—if you are attempting to get someone to choose between two things, you should shift your body just slightly in order to point your feet at the thing you would like them to choose. They are more likely to choose whatever it is you are pointing at. Likewise, if you want someone to end a conversation, you can point your feet somewhere else, such as toward a door. Most people will get the hint and move accordingly.

Chapter 13: NLP to Influence

NLP stands for neuro-lingual processing. It is an amalgamation of understanding the brain's functions, how language influences the brain's functions, and how that all impacts behaviors, which allows for people to map out their understanding of the world. Ultimately, all of the experiences that culminate into that map, which guides people through their lives. Everything someone does is guided by that map, no matter how misguided or inaccurate the map maybe. Through various methods, NLP seeks to make corrections to the flawed maps people may have developed in hopes of ensuring that the map becomes functional and accurate.

What is NLP?

NLP is a way to approach people's belief systems that allow for changes to behaviors. Through perceptual, linguistic, and behavioral techniques, such as adding new cues or using certain words, actions, and thoughts, are then changed. It is believed to be quite useful when trying to alter the behaviors of someone else and can be used in several different ways. People can use it as a therapy to work on themselves and their own behaviors, hoping to better themselves, or people can also use it as a tool to persuade or manipulate others.

Ultimately, the name refers to the nervous system (neuro), the verbal and nonverbal ways humans communicate (linguistic), and the way that we organize the neurological and linguistic input in order to get the results that are desired (processing). With those three layers, people are able to essentially tap into the minds of others with various methods and techniques in order to convince the other person to behave in other ways. It recognizes the ways that experience and communication guide all behaviors, and seeks to control it. Through controlling those, then, individuals can make huge changes in behavior.

Using NLP

Ultimately, NLP is quite broad—there are several different ways that practitioners utilize NLP in order to begin changing the minds of those around them. Each of the methods that will follow can be used in vastly different ways to get different results. With such a wide range of available techniques, everyone can find something that will work for them with relative ease, allowing for this to be quite useful for nearly everyone.

Anchoring

Anchoring is the concept that involves creating a connection between specific sensory experiences, such as a certain touch or smell, and a certain emotional state. This essentially creates a way in which people can control their own emotions. If they are, for example, prone to anger outbursts, they could anchor themselves to the feeling of calmness, tying the sensory experience of tapping their hands in a certain pattern, for example, to create that calmness artificially. This is essentially a safety net—any time they feel angry, they can tap themselves, and evoke a sense of calm rather than allowing anger to rule.

This can be used in more insidious ways as well—for example, the way the manipulator associates disobeying him with strong feels of guilt and shame that he instills in his victims.

Rapport

Rapport replies to how much a person is able to connect or relate to another, and once that connection is established, the people are far more open to feedback from each other than they would have been without the connection. This means that people are able to utilize the feedback in order to sway others to behave in ways they would not necessarily do otherwise. Oftentimes, this rapport is triggered with a combination of mirroring and empathy, in which the practitioner carefully mirrors the patient in hopes of understanding their mindsets and behaviors in order to establish the kind of relationship necessary to benefit the individual who is seeking treatment.

Of course, this can also be used by the manipulator in more insidious manners as well—the manipulator can tap into that connection through mirroring and establishing himself as trustworthy, at which point he would be able to begin messing around inside the mind of his victim. Through special attention to detail, he could begin slowly installing his own anchors within the victim that he could use later because he managed to get into that position of trust.

Swish patterns

Swish patterns refer to the technique that is used to address unwanted behaviors. It utilizes changing submodalities or the way that the behavior is approached cognitively in order to create a sort of domino effect that can completely change the behavioral patterns of the individual. Oftentimes, it takes whatever the trigger for the unwanted behavior is and seeks to override that trigger with something positive. The idea is that a trigger would then create the replacement reaction instead.

Of course, the manipulator can also take advantage of this technique, installing all sorts of behavioral patterns within his victim once he has developed the necessary rapport. Through careful attention to the words he uses and the behaviors he exhibits around his victims, he can begin to create swish patters toward serving him rather than toward constructive habits. In doing this, he essentially sets things up, so he is able to become the center of the victim's world from the inside out.

Visual/kinesthetic dissociation

Within visual/kinesthetic dissociation, the practitioner seeks to remove the negative thoughts and feelings that are associated with a trauma or other negative past event that has been causing strife for the person asking for help. Within this method, the patient is oftentimes taught to corrupt the vision of the original trauma, inserting cues that are funny or otherwise not distressing in hopes of making the person feel less upset by the negative event and more amused by it instead. This is similar to the idea of someone with stage fright imagining everyone in the audience is wearing nothing but underwear in order to alleviate the stress of speaking in front of a crowd.

Yet again, the manipulator is able to take advantage of this. It is entirely possible for the manipulator to say and do things to create negative associations with certain thoughts and feelings, ruining what may once have been a thought or concept that was calming to you instead.

Chapter 14: The Barnum Effect

Have you ever been at a fair when you are approached by a person wearing dark colors, covered in large costume jewelry, claiming that she can reach out to the dead? She may have started the conversation off with something along the lines of, "I can see him... He says he misses his bubba dearly," or something else incredibly vague. After all, most people have lost someone in their life at one point or another, and by inserting a vague nickname as well, they are likely to get someone to stop and listen. If what she says even vaguely applies to someone, especially if it is related to an emotional topic such as the loss of a loved one, the other person is likely to stop and listen, interested in what is going to happen. Even if the other person has never believed in the paranormal, a simple vague statement that could apply to most people is enough to instill doubt and draw in interest.

What is the Barnum Effect?

The Barnum effect is the effect that you see when people take something exceedingly vague and declare that it must be tailored to them. For example, imagine a horoscope—People often talk about how much of a Taurus they are because they are so stubborn, practical, and ambitious. Never mind the fact that many people can describe themselves as stubborn, practical, and ambitious, the people are wholeheartedly convinced that those vague descriptions of a person's personality are so specific that they must be trusted. This concept applies to many different paranormal instances, such as astrology, as briefly touched upon, and fortune-telling.

People will fall for vague hints at something that is clearly fishing for feedback in order to get something that could actually be utilized in a way that would be beneficial for the one attempting to manipulate others. People think that even the vaguest of hints is enough proof to legitimize whatever is being said, so long as they can at least in part identify with it.

Using the Barnum Effect to Persuade

When attempting to use the Barnum effect in order to actively persuade someone to do or believe something, you must start first with Barnum statements. These statements refer to any generalizations that could be true about the vast majority of people. Because they hold true for so many people, you can fool people into believing that you are getting a gut feeling or a paranormal sort of intuitive information.

People are more likely to believe that someone is a legitimate psychic or fortuneteller when what is said to them is even remotely related to them. This leads to a wide range of people using this effect as they convince others that they are psychic, magic, capable of communicating with the dead or even reading crystal balls, tarot cards, or palms. Any of these things, which science rejects as impossible, can be attributed to the Barnum effect.

Ultimately, psychology has studied the Barnum effect in two ways—in creating feedback for people in experiments, and in congruence with computers that are meant to give personality feedback to see whether people are more likely to believe true descriptions of themselves rather than a vague list of personality traits that could apply to nearly anyone in some capacity. In the end, it turns out that people are just as likely to accept vague, nearly meaningless descriptions than the truthfully generate personality descriptions that were actually personalized just for them.

It appears that people are much more likely to accept positive statements. People are more inclined to reject a negative statement than a positive one when it is describing an individual's personality. For example, someone is far more likely to accept something that says, "I am always stubborn and hardheaded," as accurate when contrasted with something like, "I am horrible at respecting authority."

Because people are more naturally inclined to accept positive statements, you can use positivity to counteract negative comments if you combine them. For example, you can say that someone has trouble with authority, but they use that trouble respecting the authority of others to always look for ways to better leadership positions, or to use it as a natural drive in order to encourage them to actively pursue leadership.

When you learn that people want to naturally follow vague statements that are largely positive, you can use this to your advantage, especially in a sales job. Imagine for a moment that you are a car salesperson again. A person walks in wearing sunglasses, some trendy clothing, and with a handbag that you recognize as a name brand. You instantly peg this person for someone who is likely to prefer status symbols over practicality, based on the brands that are covering her head-to-toe.

In trying to talk to her about buying a car, you then can utilize the Barnum effect to influence the woman's decision. Start with a vague comment about how much she seems to care about her appearance, leaving it just general enough that you did not imply anything serious, but leaving room for her to latch onto the idea that you understand her completely. When she is convinced that you are able to understand her and her needs, she is more likely to willingly go along with whatever it is you are suggesting at that moment. If you recommend that she gets a fancy car, she is likely to do so, and if you recommend, she gets something more practical, but spin it just right to fit with the label you have assigned, she is also likely to do so.

By utilizing the Barnum effect, you can use small tidbits that are vague to create a false understanding of the people around you, and the people you are attempting to persuade will eat it up.

Chapter 15: Cold Reading

Similarly, to the Barnum effect, cold reading is a wide range of techniques used to pretend that someone knows far more about a situation than they actually do. The person is able to look at another and gather a wide range of information at a glance, using body language, hairstyle, clothing choices, the people surrounding the individual, word choice, and basically anything else a person exudes in normal day to day interactions, and uses it to create a pretense of familiarity.

This is a technique that is oftentimes utilizing the use of highly probable guesses based solely on outside information, and that information is plenty for the individual attempting cold reading to utilize. The people that are best at this skill are typically quite perceptive, paying close attention to body language in order to understand how close they are too convincing the other person, or whether the effort will be largely wasted if a particular line of questioning is kept up.

Oftentimes, people are quick to fall for this due to their own confirmation biases. With those biases, they feel that vague comments are accurate, even when they are so vague that they apply to several other people around them. The propensity to fall for these vague statements comes from humanity's deep-seated need and desire to find meaning in everything, as well as the hope of being able to communicate with someone lost in the future. People will often jump at the idea that they can speak to someone they have lost, and con artists love to manipulate this fact, taking advantage in order to get as much money as possible from the poor suckers who never bothered to research their actions or the efficacy of such acts. They essentially take advantage of the poor people's desperation for their own selfish reasons and run with it, convincing the other person of something that is not true simply for some easy money.

Uses of Cold Reading

Ultimately, cold reading is largely used as a scam. People who are particularly good at understanding and reading others will utilize this sort of cold reading in order to earn money, taking advantage of those who are not smart enough to realize that it is a scam. The con artist that utilizes cold reading, then, is able to essentially fool another person into believing that the artist is capable of far more than he or she actually is, and in doing so, earns the trust of the other person.

Cold reading can be used persuasively as well, such as in the previously discussed example with the car salesperson in the Barnum effect chapter. When you are able to cold read well, you can oftentimes convince people that you are particularly good at reading people, which allows for a deepening in trust that allows the other person to feel as though you are trustworthy, even though you have done nothing but scam them. By utilizing confirmation biases, in which people are always more likely to see themselves in vague descriptions, and offer any information the con artist would need to continue the con.

How to Use Cold Reading

Ultimately, there are several different kinds of cold readings, with the Barnum effect included within them. In this section, you will take a look at several of the most effective methods of cold reading. Through learning these methods, you will begin to understand just how people actually fall for these cons.

Likewise, in understanding that these cons exist, you are far more likely to be able to protect yourself in the future.

Shotgunning

In shotgunning, the con artist starts with something incredibly vague, and oftentimes even leads with a declaration of how vague the art can be. For example, the con artist may say, "Now, this is often more meaningful for you than it is for me, so please, feel free to help me help you." This does two things— it sets the individual up to expect vagueness that will need to be applied later, and it also tells the individual being conned that they should trust the artist, specifically by appealing to the likability principle of working toward a common goal.

From there, the artist will shoot out several vague comments in quick succession, watching closely for any signs of recognition or reactions in the person that is being conned. They may say something about someone beyond the grave attempting to contact the individual and then wait for the individual's reaction to tell the story. Over time, the artist continues to fire more and more at the individual, slowly homing in on something that is specific. Over time, between studying the reactions of the other person and through making sure that everything is vague enough that it could be applicable, the individual is able to convince the other person that he or she can communicate with the dead.

Fishing

In fishing, things are slightly more methodical than shotgunning, but it is still entirely dependent on reading the victim and understanding the victim's reactions as they occur. In this type of cold reading, the con artist starts with a vague, but educated guess about the victim. Based off of looking at them, the con artist can decide what kind of position the victim may be in, and then begin fishing for information. For example, if it is a middle-aged person, they may begin with a comment about someone standing behind the individual. The con artist may throw in a different hint, such as asking whether the other person has lost a parent or grandparent recently while watching closely to see how the other person reacts. Even if the other person tries not to, some subtle behavioral cues can occur, leading the person to continue fishing. The con artist may then move on to attempting to guess the cause of death or circumstances around the death, oftentimes saying that the person is gesturing to an area that is often full of complications. The fisher essentially convinces the victim through these vague comments and cons the person out of money.

Rainbow Ruse

When using the rainbow ruse, a con artist takes traits of the Barnum effect and applies them with contradictions. By listing off common personality traits while also pairing it with the opposite, the con artist is then able to rope in virtually anyone on the spectrum. For example, the con artist may say something along the lines of, "While you are most kind and compassionate to those around you, there was a time recently when someone hurt you badly enough that you did something you regret." This is such a vague statement that it could apply to virtually everyone. There is not likely to be a single person alive that has not done something in anger that was not shortly after regretted, and the con artist knows this. With these vague statements, the con artist is able to convince the other person that he understands the other person.

Warm Reading

Warm reading is slightly different than cold reading, in which the con artist has enough vague information to have a general idea as to where to aim for with cold reading techniques, putting him a step ahead of the cold reader. It often involves someone who has a general idea of how psychology and statistics work, and the warm reader will utilize those to his advantage.

For example, he understands that people often keep mementos of people we have lost that has some sort of significance, such as an accessory that the person often wore, as well as the leading causes of death within the country. The reader will often use those leading causes of death as ways to fish for information about how the individual died, as well as hinting at people having a piece of jewelry or a watch that belonged to the deceased. By hinting at those and recognizing how to read someone, the warm reader is able to work with more efficiency than the cold reader to the same end.

Chapter 16: Mirroring

Have you ever sat in a restaurant and people watched? It can be quite amusing to sit back and watch all of the people out and about around you, attempting to identify how their relationships must be going by body language alone. Yes, it is quite possible to understand at the briefest glance at another how they get along. You can absolutely tell how much or how little people get along simply by watching them together and seeing how they naturally orient their bodies around each other. This simple skill is referred to as mirroring, and it is absolutely crucial if you want to be successful at influencing or persuading others. When you understand mirroring, you essentially have a built-in system in which you can judge just how well people are likely to be willing to listen to you. You can tell if you are successful in developing rapport, and if you have not, you will be able to push the act of earning rapport along a little quicker. You can utilize mirroring in a wide range of ways that can absolutely be beneficial to you, and you can utilize it in ways that can be useful to others as well.

What is Mirroring?

First things first, you must learn what mirroring is. At the simplest, it is the human tendency to mirror what is happening around them when they feel a relationship to whatever it is that is around them. For example, if you look at an old married couple, they are likely to constantly be mirroring each other's behaviors. It is essentially the ultimate culmination of empathy—the individuals are so bonded, so aware of each other and their behaviors, that they unconsciously mimic any behaviors that their partner does first. The two married people at the diner may both sip at their coffees at the same time as each other, or if one drinks, the other will follow shortly after. If one shifts in his seat, she will do so as well, always leaning to mirror the position her husband is in. If she brushes off something on her shoulder, he will unconsciously touch his shoulder as well. This act is known as mirroring, and it occurs in a wide range of circumstances.

You do not necessarily have to be a married couple that has been together for decades for mirroring to be relevant, either— you can see it everywhere. The person interviewing you for a job may begin to mirror you when the interview is going well, or the person who thinks that you are attractive may mimic some of your behaviors as well. You can see these behaviors mimicked started quite early on in terms of how long people have been interacting as well—sometimes people will even hit it off right off the bat and begin mirroring each other, emphasizing the fact that they seemed to have clicked.

Mirroring is essentially the ultimate form of flattery—it involves literally copying the other person because you like or love them so much. Children mirror their parents when learning how to behave in the world. Good friends often mirror each other. Salespeople wanting to win rapport, mirror people. No matter what the relationship is, if it is a positive one, there are likely mirroring behaviors, whether unconscious or not.

Uses of Mirroring

You may be wondering why something as simple as mimicry can actually be important to others, but it is actually one of the most fundamental parts of influence, persuasion, and manipulation. When you mirror someone, you can develop rapport. Rapport is essentially the measurement of your relationship with someone—if you have a good rapport with someone, you have developed some level of trust with them.

The other person is likely to believe what you are saying if you develop rapport. However, if you have not yet developed rapport yet and you need the other person to listen to you, you can oftentimes artificially create that rapport through one simple task—mirroring. If you mirror the other person, you can essentially convince him to develop a rapport with you, whether it was something he wanted to develop on his own or whether you forced the point.

By constantly mirroring the other person, you essentially send the signs to their brain that they need to like this person because this person is just like them. Remember the three key factors for likability? The first one was able to relate or identify with the other person. In this case, you are presenting yourself as easy to relate to simply because you want the other person to like you. With liking you comes rapport. With rapport comes trust, which you can use to convince the other person to buy cars, or do certain things that will benefit you. Building rapport even builds up the ability to be able to manipulate the other person—you need to be trustworthy for the other person to let you close enough to manipulate in the first place.

How to Mirror

Luckily for you, mirroring is quite easy to learn how to do. While it may seem awkward and unnatural at first, the more you practice it, the more natural it will become to you, and the more effective you can get at it. Remember, if you want to mirror someone, you will need to toe the line between too much and not enough. If you are too overt, the other person will catch on and will likely be more put off than convinced to like you. Take a look at these four steps so you can learn to mirror for yourself.

Build up a Connection

The first step when you are attempting to mirror someone is to start by building a connection somehow. If you do not feel the connection with the other person, they are not likely to be feeling a connection either. Keeping that in mind, you should begin to foster some sort of connection and rapport. This can be done with four simple steps on its own.

- **Fronting**: This is the act of facing the other person entirely. You start with your body oriented toward them, directly facing the other person to give them your complete attention.
- **Eye contact**: This is the tricky part—when you are making eye contact, you need to make sure that you get the right amount. See the steps provided in the earlier section on eye contact to make sure you get this part right.
- **The triple nod:** This does two things—it encourages the other person to keep speaking because the other person feels valued and listened to, and it makes the other person feel like you agree with them. It develops what is known as a yes set. The more you say yes, the more likely you are to develop a connection with the other person.
- **Fake it till you make it:** At this point, you have spent a lot of time setting up the connection, and it is time for the moment of truth. You should imagine that the person is the most interesting in the world at that particular moment. You want to really believe that they are interesting to you. Then stop pretending—you should feel that they are actually interesting to you at this point. This is the birth of the connection you had been trying to establish.

Pace and Volume

Now, before you start mimicking their body language, start by paying attention to the other person's vocal cues. You want to make sure you are speaking at the same speed as the other person. If they are a quick speaker, you should also speak quickly, and if they are a slower speaker, you should slow your own speaking pace down to match. From there, make sure you are also mimicking the volume. If they are louder, you should raise your own voice. If they are keeping their voice down, you should follow suit. These vocal cues are far easier to mimic undetected than the rest of the physical cues.

The Punctuator

Everyone has a punctuator they use for emphasis. It could be something like a hand gesture that is used every time they want to emphasize something, or it could be the way they raise their brows as they say the word they want to stress. No matter what the punctuator is, you should identify what it is and seek to mimic it at the moment. Now, oftentimes, this cue is entirely unconscious on the other person's part, and as you begin to mimic it, the other person is likely to believe that you are on the same wavelength. This should really do it for you without making what you are doing obviously.

The Moment of Truth

Now, you are ready to test whether you have successfully built up the rapport you need. When you want to know if the other person has officially been connected to you, you should make some small action that is unrelated to what you are doing at that particular moment and see if the other person does it back. For example, if you are having a conversation about computers, you may reach up and rub your forehead for a split second. Watch and see if the other person also rubs at their forehead right after you. If they do, they have connected to you, and you can begin to move forward with your persuasive techniques.

Chapter 17: Tips for Dealing with Manipulation

10 Tips for Dealing with Manipulators

Cut Them Off

When you are attempting to avoid the manipulator's antics, perhaps the most successful is by entirely removing them from your life like the malignant cancer they are. In completely separating yourself from the manipulator, you will find yourself far happier, rediscovering yourself and your own thoughts and beliefs that have been suppressed all this time thanks to the manipulator's actions. You will be more successful, more capable of dealing with life, and infinitely happier without that toxicity constantly raining on your parade.

Ignore, Ignore, Ignore!

Manipulators want you to follow along with whatever they want you to do. They will say whatever it takes to get that reaction from you, even if their methods are cruel or hurtful. They may even make it a point to say things that you know to be blatantly untrue in hopes of getting you to react negatively or attempt to correct it. For example, they may make a snide comment to you, such as asking when the next baby is due. You could correct the person, calling out their awful behavior, or you could ignore it.

Think about it this way—when you make it a point to fight back, you are giving them exactly what they want. You are reacting emotionally, which means that the strings that he installed are still firmly in place, which allows them to continue to manipulate you. They can continue to poke and prod at you, hoping to make you more and more upset while they learn all about your triggers that can be used against you in the future. If ignoring is not an option at that particular moment, you can choose to instead not react or agree with whatever is said just to get the other person to stop. By removing the emotions, you do not reward the manipulator's behaviors.

Trust Yourself

Manipulators thrive off of convincing you that you do not know what is best. They may even go out of their ways to make you doubt your own perceptions of the world, convincing you that you are wrong about inane details about life until you are so convinced that you cannot see the world clearly that you default to the manipulator's decisions. Instead of listening to what the manipulator says is best for you, it is time to take back the control and trust yourself.

Look at your own desires. Look at your own opinions. They are valid and worthy of pursuing. You should not allow for the manipulator in your life to make decisions that have very little impact on him or her. Do not allow him or her to define you and follow your own values. After all, you are ultimately the best judge of what is best for you. Those beliefs that you have are acceptable, and no one should be able to take them away from you.

Beat the Manipulator at His Own Game

Manipulators love to sneak into your life and slowly take it all over. They will take over your friends before systematically turning them against you. They may choose to point out how much of a failure you are because of some past mistake that is no longer relevant to anything you are doing just to put you down. They may find something that you want and constantly keep it just out of your reach for their own selfish thrills.

Sometimes, if nothing else works and even ignoring the manipulator is not effective, going on the offensive is the next best thing. In this case, you need to identify the one thing the manipulator has that he wants to keep close. It could be a person, a position, or a skill. No matter what it is, discover what it is, and attempt to overthrow the manipulator. If he has a friend that he actually values, befriend that person. If he is in a position because he is skilled at something and you happen to share that skillset, make it a point to take his position. Ultimately, as you take over part of his life, you will leave him scrambling to put his own life back together, essentially freeing you while his focus shifts.

Break the Habit

Sometimes, you get so caught up in status quo that, even if you want to separate from a manipulator, you cannot get yourself out of the rut. You may find yourself suddenly missing the manipulator in your life, or something may happen that triggers a reaction that you did not expect. When this happens, recognize that the best step is to step out of your comfort zone and break the habits you have developed surrounding the manipulator. This does two things—it breaks your habituated response to obeying whatever the manipulator has conditioned you to do, and it also shows the manipulator that you are no longer going to tolerate the manipulator's whims. The next time you feel the need to give in to what the narcissist expects, then, you should attempt to try something new.

Do Not Expect Them to Agree with You

While you may hope that the manipulator will be rational if you try to speak to them or tell them how you are feeling like normal, rational humans would do, you cannot expect the manipulator to actually learn anything from a confrontation. Instead, the manipulator will see it as ammo to use against you in any way possible rather than as something that could be used as a learning experience. Instead of hoping that you can change the manipulator, cut your losses and move on. You will be far happier if you do so.

Do Not Give in To Guilt

Guilt can be incredibly powerful—in fact, it is so powerful, it was likely used by the manipulator against you several times. Manipulators recognize the driving power of guilt when obligations are not met, and they utilize it well. However, you should not feel guilty for not living up to the manipulator's standards. You do not have to give in to the manipulator, nor do you have to give in to the manipulator's attempts to make you feel bad. Remember, recognize your innate human rights and utilize them. You are allowed to say no without feeling guilty.

Never Ask for Permission

You are your own person. You do not need to ask the manipulator for permission to do something, nor should you ever feel the urge to do so. Instead of being concerned with the feelings of others, you should instead focus on disempowering the manipulator. He can only control you if you let him, and one of the ways you would hand over power is if you asked for permission.

If the Manipulator Is Getting Confrontational, Attempt to Defuse the Situation and Leave

An angered manipulator is never a good one, and he may lash out in ways that you would not have expected. If you can sense that the situation is growing heated, you need to figure out a way to disengage and leave without causing a nuclear explosion. You can do this in several ways, but the most effective is by shutting it down firmly without giving the opportunity for a comeback. For example, if you have someone attempting to convince you that their corrupted version of what happened last week is accurate, you can simply tell them that you remember things differently and that you would like some time away to consider their perspective, and then walk away. By doing this quickly and firmly, the manipulator is stuck.

Insistence That You Will Not Continue a Discussion While the Other Person Is Emotional

Oftentimes, as manipulators feel their grasp over a situation slipping away, they will begin to react explosively or emotionally in a last-ditch effort to convince you to stick around. There may be screaming, threats of self-harm, or of harming you, throwing things, or other violence. In this situation, remember two things—the first is that if you feel as though you are in danger, then you need to disengage and contact authorities as soon as possible. Secondly, realize that you are not responsible for the other person's emotional state, no matter how much he may try to convince you that you are. Telling him firmly that you refuse to have a conversation when he is so upset and walking away is probably the simplest way to end the argument without allowing him to feel.

10 Tips for Becoming Less Vulnerable to Exploitation

Learn the Signs

The easiest way to protect yourself is through ensuring you know how to recognize the signs of manipulators. Congratulations! You have already done this by reading through this book! As you learn what to look for, you know when something does not look right, and you will be able to question the other person, which brings us to tip #2--

Never Ignore the Red Flags

You should NEVER ignore any red flags about the other person. If they are behaving in manipulative ways and you recognize that, you should not try to make excuses or give the other person the benefit of the doubt—he does not deserve it if he is manipulating you. Do not give in to any sob stories or anything else said to convince you to give in, and instead, focus on the fact that you deserve better.

Focus on Self-Care

The manipulator will look for people who do not value themselves. Those who do not see their own inherent value are typically much easier at manipulating into doing what they desire simply because they do not think they deserve better, and when they feel like they do not deserve better, they are not likely to resist the manipulation, even when it hurts them. By focusing on self-care, you are telling yourself that you are valuable. You are giving yourself the care you deserve to ensure that you are healthy and cared for, which makes you less desirable. While most people will find confidence attractive, the manipulator wants nothing to do with it.

Develop Self-Esteem

This might be easier said than done, but it is still relevant—you should always seek out ways to develop your own self-esteem. When you do, you will find that you are a much happier and healthier individual. That alone will make you less attractive to the manipulator for the same reasons that focusing on self-care will make you less attractive.

Make a Support Network

The easiest targets are those who are already isolated or are easy to isolate. By surrounding yourself with a network of friends, family, and even a support group that pertains to the victims of manipulators could do wonders in terms of protecting you in the future. The more people around you, the more roadblocks the manipulator sees to get you under control.

Better Yourself

Also similar to develop self-esteem and engaging in self-care, you should seek to better yourself in some way. Go back to school for that degree you have always wanted, or go to the gym and get yourself in better shape. You could learn a new skill, such as baking or fishing, or begin hiking or volunteering. Find something that you are passionate about and pour yourself into it to better yourself. No one ever regrets acting in ways to better themselves, and it will be a welcome distraction from dealing with the manipulator.

Never Settle

Recognize that you are no less deserving of happiness and health than anyone else. You are absolutely deserving of a good relationship, of being respected, and living a happy life, free of abuse and manipulation. You can achieve this through respecting yourself—never settle for someone who is giving you less than the best. The people you surround yourself with should see your value and want you to be the best you that you can be, without feeling the need to change you or manipulate you. You should seek out only people who will help you achieve your goals in life without hindering you, or who will always be there to encourage you rather than cut you down during the tough times. You should never feel the need to settle for a relationship or friendship that is less than you deserve.

Set Boundaries and Keep Them at All Costs

One of the keys to minimizing your exploitability is through boundaries. Boundaries are essentially shielding between yourself and the manipulator, and while the manipulator will attempt to bang on that shield in hopes of it shattering, you must have the faith necessary that it will not crack under the manipulator's attempts. Trust yourself and your boundaries, and always honor them. Do not drop your boundaries because they felt too heavy to hold at that moment. You need to make sure you are keeping them up to protect yourself and to prove to the manipulator that they are non-negotiable, even if that is the hard way to getting what you want.

Trust the Judgment of Your Friends and Family

Pay attention to how those around you react to people you invite into your life. If they seem to feel that the person is showing red flags, you should seriously consider their perspectives. They may be onto something—there could be some serious problems that you are overlooking, whether due to infatuation or any other reasons that are keeping you interested in following the manipulator.

Remember That If It Seems Too Good to Be True, It Probably Is

Manipulators sneak their ways into the lives of their victims through pretending to be someone they are not. They are masters at pretending to be someone desirable and wanted in order to convince people to let them in. So many people find themselves feeling like they are lucky to have the manipulator in their lives because of how they initially present themselves, but over time, they let their true selves out. They know that no one would want to be around them if they knew the truth, and they hide it for that reason. It is just another part of their manipulation attempts. Do not give them that power and do not entertain it.

Conclusion

Congratulations! You have made it to the end of this book. Hopefully, the process was beneficial to you as you made your way through all of the information this book had to offer you. Within this book, you were given a plethora of information necessary to understanding the secrets of dark psychology and recognizing the vast majority of ways that dark psychology can be used in both ethical and unethical manners.

Within this book, you were treated with a wide variety of topics, ranging from background information about emotions and empathy all the way to various ways people can use to manipulate others, along with everything in between. These pages have sought to provide you with all of the information you could possibly need in order to recognize and avoid manipulation for your own safety and sanity. Ultimately, most manipulators have absolutely no qualms about manipulating others and are glad to do so if it means that they get what they want. Their only real concern is in helping themselves and ensuring someone is meeting their needs.

As you read, you were given several pages of relevant information for you to master. Ultimately, the most important pieces of information for you to take away from this entire book lie in understanding the value of ethics and how to treat others ethically, recognizing the nonverbal communication of others, and recognizing how to protect yourself from the manipulation of others.

As you continue forward on your journey through dark psychology, learning to navigate through the darkness, you are now armed with several tools that will protect you. You will see now how to ensure you are safe at all costs. You will see the signs that you or those around you are being manipulated, and you will have the skills to handle that manipulation with ease. From here, consider this book and the information within it a valuable guide. If you ever feel a need to brush up on the basics, come back here. This can be your grounding point as you continue to delve deeper into the arts of dark psychology. Remember to keep ethics at the forefront of your mind, and that you do not have to fall into the darkness just because you have taken a look at what it has to offer. You can utilize the concepts of dark psychology without hurting anyone.

This book absolutely is not intended for you to use to manipulate or hurt other people. It is intended as an educational guide that will provide valuable insight into the strange and dark minds of those who manipulate the most. With that understanding, the possibilities within the world are endless. From here, your next step is to start looking at individual strategies and concepts behind various types of persuasion and manipulation. You have all of the background information now to move forward and further your understanding. Good luck on your journey into understanding the darkness.

Printed in Great Britain
by Amazon